Tribute to Henry A. "Hank" Rosso

THIS WORKBOOK SERIES is dedicated to the legacy of Henry A. "Hank" Rosso, noted by many experts as one of the leading figures in the development of organized philanthropic fund raising in the twentieth century. This series of workbooks, ranging from *Making Your Case for Support* to *Building Your Endowment*, was the last project he undertook before his health failed him. The Indiana University Center on Philanthropy, of which he was a founder, is honored to have been asked to complete this project on Hank's behalf. My colleagues and I dedicate this series to his memory.

I am grateful to my colleague Tim Seiler for agreeing to serve as editor. Tim is director of The Fund Raising School, the national and international training program that Hank started in 1974. It is appropriate that this workbook series be tied directly to concepts and materials taught by The Fund Raising School.

By carefully studying the practitioners and scholars in fund raising who came before him, Hank was able to codify and teach principles and techniques for effective philanthropic fund raising. Scores of practitioners who applied his principles have been successful in diversifying their philanthropic fund raising and donor bases in sustaining their worthy causes. Hank was constantly concerned that those who might most need the information of The Fund Raising School might least be able to access it. He developed special courses for small organizations and edited *Achieving Excellence in Fund Raising* to get information into the hands of practitioners. This workbook series was for Hank another attempt to put the tools of effective philanthropic fund raising into the hands of practitioners who could not get to The Fund Raising School courses.

We hope you find this material useful to you in your work. One of Hank's favorite sayings was, "You can raise a lot more money with organized fund raising than you can with disorganized fund raising." We hope it helps you organize and find success in your fund raising activities. As you carry out your work, remember Hank's definition: "Fund raising is the gentle art of teaching the joy of giving."

Eugene R. Tempel
Executive Director
Indiana University Center on Philanthropy

FORTHCOMING BOOKS IN THE EXCELLENCE IN FUND RAISING WORKBOOK SERIES:

Planning Special Events

Developing Your Case for Support

Setting Up Your Annual Fund

Building Your Direct Mail Program

Building Your Endowment

OTHER NONPROFIT RESOURCES FROM JOSSEY-BASS:

The Five Strategies for Fundraising Success, Mal Warwick

Conducting a Successful Capital Campaign, Second Edition, Kent E. Dove

Winning Grants Step by Step, Mim Carlson

The Fundraising Planner: A Working Model for Raising the Dollars You Need, Terry and Doug Schaff

The Jossey-Bass Guide to Strategic Communications for Nonprofits, Kathy Bonk, Henry Griggs, Emily Tynes

Marketing Nonprofit Programs and Services, Douglas B. Herron

Transforming Fundraising: A Practical Guide to Evaluating and Strengthening Fundraising to Grow with Change, Judith E. Nichols

Achieving Excellence in Fund Raising, Henry A. Rosso and Associates

The Grantwriter's Start-Up Kit, Successful Images, Inc.

Secrets of Successful Grantsmanship, Susan L. Golden

The Excellence in Fund Raising Workbook Series

WORKBOOK SERIES

THE FUND RAISING WORKBOOK SERIES began with Hank Rosso and his vision of a set of separate yet interrelated workbooks designed to offer practical, high-quality models for successful fund raising. Each workbook focuses on a single topic and provides narrative material explaining the topic, worksheets, sample materials, and other practical advice. Designed and written for fund raising professionals, nonprofit leaders, and volunteers, the workbooks provide models and strategies for carrying out successful fund raising programs. The texts are based on the accumulated experience and wisdom of veteran fund raising professionals as validated by research, theory, and practice. Each workbook stands alone yet is part of a bigger whole. The workbooks are similar in format and design and use as their primary textual content the curriculum of The Fund Raising School as originally developed and written by Hank Rosso, Joe Mixer, and Lyle Cook. Hank selected or suggested authors for the series and intended to be coeditor of the series. The authors stay true to Hank's philosophy of fund raising, and the series is developed as a form of stewardship to Hank's ideals of ethical fund raising. All authors address how their contributions to the series act in tandem with the other steps in Hank's revolutionary Fund Raising Cycle, as illustrated here. It is the intent of the editor and of the publisher that this will be the premier hands-on workbook series for fund raisers and their volunteers.

The Fund Raising School
Dedicated to the advancement of ethical fund raising

Timothy L. Seiler

General Series Editor

Director, The Fund Raising School

Indiana University Center on Philanthropy

The Fund Raising Cycle

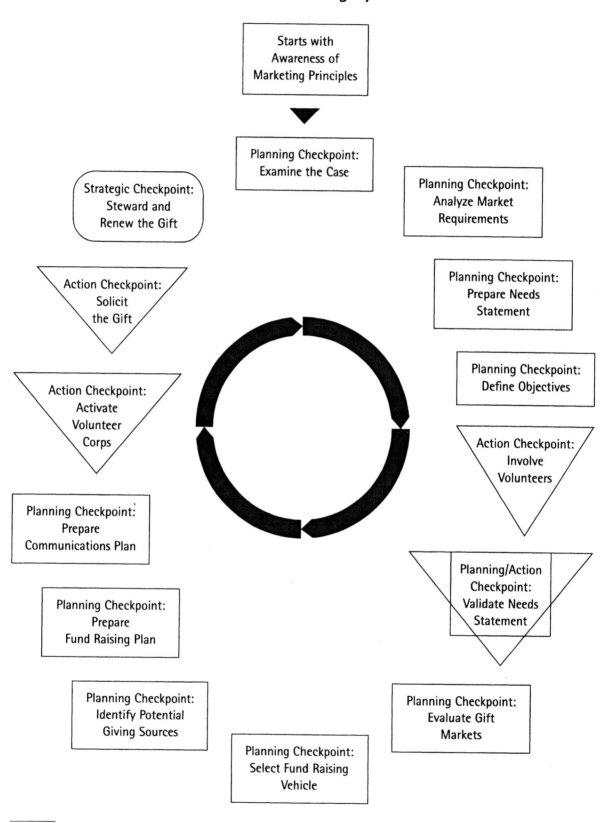

PREPARING YOUR CAPITAL CAMPAIGN

EXCELLENCE IN
FUND RAISING

WORKBOOK SERIES

Series Editor
Timothy L. Seiler

PREPARING
YOUR CAPITAL
CAMPAIGN

MARILYN BANCEL

JOSSEY-BASS
A Wiley Company
San Francisco

Jossey-Bass books and products are available through most bookstores. To contact Jossey-Bass directly, call (888) 378-2537, fax to (800) 605-2665, or visit our website at www.josseybass.com.

Substantial discounts on bulk quantities of Jossey-Bass books are available to corporations, professional associations, and other organizations. For details and discount information, contact the special sales department at Jossey-Bass.

Library of Congress Cataloging-in-Publication Data

Bancel, Marilyn, date.
    Preparing your capital campaign / Marilyn Bancel.—1st ed.
        p. cm. — (The Jossey-Bass nonprofit and public management
series)
    ISBN 0-7879-5247-8 (acid-free paper)
    1. fund raising. 2. Nonprofit organizations—Finance. I. Title.
II. Series.
  HG177 .B36 2000
  658.15'224—dc21
                          00-010234

PB Printing 10 9 8 7 6 5 4 3 2 1   FIRST EDITION

The Jossey-Bass
Nonprofit and Public Management Series

Contents

Preface   xv

The Author   xix

Introduction: Why Take the Time to Prepare?   1

1. **Understanding the Capital Campaign   5**

What Is a Capital Campaign?   5

Forms of Capital Campaigns   5

Examples of Capital Projects   6

The Stages of a Campaign   7

Do You Really Need a Capital Campaign?   7

When Should Your Organization Undertake a Capital Campaign?   9

What's in a Goal?   12

Does Your Organization Cope Well with Risk?   13

2. **Getting the Organization Ready   17**

Telling Your Story   17

Putting Strong Volunteer Leadership in Place   20

Evaluating Your Donor and Prospect Base   27

Preparing Your Institutional Plan   43

Getting Professional Support in Place   47

Establishing Effective Communications Channels   51

Establishing Visibility   58

Paying for Building Your Organization's Capacity   60

3. Launching the Project 63

Testing for Project Readiness 63

Developing a Rationale for the Project 65

Getting Buy-In and Commitment from Internal Constituencies 67

Getting Ready for a Bricks-and-Mortar Project 69

What Costs Will We Encounter and When? 70

Obtaining Up-Front Planning Costs 73

Answering Important Questions 74

Understanding the Role of In-Kind Donations 77

4. Conducting a Feasibility Study 79

What Is a Feasibility Study? 80

Do You Need a Study? 80

What You Can Learn from a Study 82

How to Get Ready for a Feasibility Study 83

How to Time the Study 90

How to Find the Right Consultant 91

Cost of a Feasibility Study 93

Risks of Not Undertaking a Study 94

Alternatives to a Feasibility Study 95

5. Building the Campaign Framework 99

Responding to the Results of the Feasibility Study 99

Deciding Next Steps 100

Setting a Campaign Goal 101

Preparing the Case Statement 103

Posing Questions to Leadership 106

Using the Test to Prepare for Volunteer Training 108

Thanking and Acknowledging Participants 108

6. Raising Early Funding 111

Determine Early Funding Needs 111

Option One: Campaign for a Seed Fund 112

Option Two: Build a Campaign Chest 113

Option Three: Establish a Loan Fund 114

Option Four: Establish a Combination Leadership Fund and Loan Fund 114

Option Five: Use Public Bond Funds or Tax-Exempt Financing 114

Option Six: Use Private Bond Funds 115

Option Seven: Get Creative 115

7. **Looking Ahead 117**

Resources 119

Top Ten Reasons Campaigns Fail 120

Estimating the Costs of Fund Raising 121

Sample Expenses for a Three-Year $3 Million Capital Campaign 124

Organizations 125

References 127

Useful Publications 129

Dedicated to
Henry A. "Hank" Rosso
(1918–1999),
great teacher, great lover of
humanity, who urged us all to
"show others how to give proudly
and be happy for their gifts"

Preface

THIS IS A BOOK about getting ready for a capital campaign. When Henry A. "Hank" Rosso, founder of The Fund Raising School, asked me to undertake the writing of a workbook on capital campaigns for Jossey-Bass Publishers, I saw that as being a fairly straightforward project. My editor, however, on seeing the outline, correctly noted that the preparatory section constituted an entire book in itself. That "preparatory section" thus became *Preparing Your Capital Campaign.*

This workbook focuses on the steps leading up to a campaign—but probably not all the steps you will need to take. The experienced fund raiser may look for planning steps that are not here. That is because the line between the preparation stage and the final planning stage is no line at all. It's a period of about six months. Chapter Seven, the last chapter, offers a look ahead at what comes during that planning time, which is actually the start-up phase of the campaign.

Please be advised that no workbook can substitute for some of the excellent comprehensive texts available on the subject of preparing for and implementing a capital campaign. See especially *Conducting a Successful Capital Campaign* (2nd edition) by Kent E. Dove (Jossey-Bass, 2000). Use the chapters here as a step-by-step companion to such a book. Other relevant works are listed in the Useful Publications section at the end of the book.

Audience for the Book

This workbook speaks primarily to the development professional with executive responsibilities in an organization and to executive directors who must build their organization's fund raising strengths. It can also help volunteers who want to understand what needs to precede a campaign and how they might help strengthen their organization. (See especially Chapter Five.) The tools in this book, however, are meant for the entire organization.

For newcomers to the subject, Chapter One provides a rapid overview of a capital campaign. With so many moving parts, campaigns are a challenge to describe quickly enough to potential campaigners with an avid interest. Chapter One both presents the basics and helps answer some key "go" or "no-go" questions.

The remainder of the workbook is based on the assumption that the reader has had enough development experience to be familiar with basic terminology and fund raising practice. Long-time professionals may find the book most helpful as a reminder set of checklists and gap-fillers, as most will have walked these roads already.

How Will This Book Help You?

If you have never been through a capital campaign before, you will find the start-from-scratch approach in this workbook particularly helpful. When you look at preparation in detail, many steps emerge, and their order is important. The chapters will help you learn what the tasks are and show you how to put them in proper sequence. It is tempting to put the cart before the horse; that's easy to do if you don't know what "cart" and "horse" mean in campaignese.

The preparation phase is crucial because the organization must prepare *by itself* in order to build up strength. For some organizations the process can take years. Organizations that have institutionalized annual planning and board-strengthening activities will find themselves much closer to the starting line. If an organization has not completed the basic steps toward readiness, as outlined in this book, no consultant—not even a fleet of fund raisers—can manufacture a successful campaign. Either you do the homework and have a campaign or you have a few friends who will always send over quantities of stock on request, thus rendering a campaign moot.

Where Does This Book Fit into the Fund Raising Cycle?

Experienced fund raisers will be familiar with the term *fund raising cycle*, which describes the set of activities needed to prepare for, cultivate, obtain, and steward a gift. Hank Rosso was fond of diagramming the cycle in fourteen steps.

The exercises in this workbook walk you through nine steps of the cycle—all of the getting-ready steps for a capital campaign. In Rosso's terms, those steps include the following (Rosso and Associates, 1991, p. 10):

- Examine the case.

- Define objectives.

- Prepare a needs statement (strategic planning and capital needs planning encompass these first three steps).

- Analyze market requirements (learn who your donor market really is and what they need and want).

- Involve volunteers (crucial).

- Validate needs statement (this is accomplished through a feasibility study).

- Evaluate gift markets (this is also done by way of a feasibility study).

- Select a fund raising vehicle (include the type of campaign, recognition program, and more).

- Identify potential giving sources (this is an ongoing feature).

Campaign planning and implementation is not addressed in this workbook, but information that is currently available in the books referenced here address the next five steps:

- Prepare the fund raising plan.

- Prepare a communications plan (you get a good head start in this book).

- Expand the volunteer corps (you'll start that here as well).

- Solicit the gift.

- Renew the gift (go through all the steps again).

Will this book substitute for wisdom and good judgment? I hope not. But technical, step-by-step guidance in a workbook of this type can help with direction. In the meantime, the hard work of getting people to work together well must go forward. In the preface to his book, *High-Impact Consulting,* author Robert H. Schaffer (1997) observes, "Mountains of data indicate that only rarely is not knowing what to do the greatest obstacle to organizational success" (p.6). In these pages I have attempted to show exactly what an organization needs to do to prepare for a capital campaign. The factors underlying a successful campaign, however, reach to the deepest levels of organizational health.

The following pages and quizzes describe the steps an organization needs to take to prepare a campaign. It will be up to you and perhaps your consultants to help your organization move forward with these steps. When you do so, you may find that no matter what the outcome of a campaign, your organization will be able to function better and serve better and will enable you to feel the joy of accomplishment in a world that needs you.

Acknowledgments

My lasting thanks for what I have learned and can pass along in this book go to the two great Hanks of American fund raising—Henry A. Rosso, founder of The Fund Raising School, and Henry Goldstein, president and CEO of The Oram Group, Inc., the well-known and long-established consulting firm to philanthropic organizations. I am also indebted to former colleagues Charles Ries and Virginia Carollo Rubin for wisdom and balance. For their insightful and invaluable reading of the draft manuscript, I thank my colleague Mary Schmidt and the wonderful editors and readers at Jossey-Bass Publishers. And ever, thank you Rik, Carey, and Roxanne.

San Francisco, California   Marilyn Bancel
July 2000

The Author

MARILYN BANCEL is vice president of The Oram Group, Inc.—a national fund raising and nonprofit consulting firm serving philanthropic organizations since 1940. Based in San Francisco, where she has lived since 1972, Bancel anchors Oram's West Coast operations, consulting to a wide variety of nonprofit organizations. She has a special perspective on the needs of fund raising staff, having spent fifteen of her twenty-five years in the field as a development director. In addition to her consulting, Bancel is adjunct professor at the University of San Francisco's Institute of Nonprofit Management where she teaches Capital Campaigns and Major Gifts—a course originally developed by Hank Rosso. She frequently conducts fund raising seminars and conference workshops.

PREPARING YOUR CAPITAL CAMPAIGN

Introduction
Why Take the Time to Prepare?

VERY FEW ENDEAVORS offer as much challenge, as much exhilaration, and as much satisfaction as a capital campaign. The stakes, the risks, and the rewards are all great. Embarking on a campaign can be both thrilling and nerve-racking.

Proper preparation will both anchor you and protect you from potentially costly mistakes. "When a capital campaign truly succeeds," says John E. Marshall III, president of The Kresge Foundation (1994), "it leaves in its wake a stronger board and a giving constituency that is broader and deeper. Both will be useful to the organization when it faces the inevitable challenges and opportunities that occur when *not* in a capital campaign."

You should read Chapter One closely if your organization is inexperienced in campaigning. The chapter provides a good overview of the many moving parts needed to prepare for a capital campaign without your having to work through the entire book to see how the parts fit together.

Taking the time to prepare pays off. Rushing into a campaign can set your organization back instead of advancing it. If your goal is too ambitious or relies too heavily on a wobbly infrastructure, you invite any number of mishaps. Conversely, if your vision is too narrow, if you wait too long to pursue it, or your goal is too modest, you may fail to capture imaginations and hearts and end by falling short. Lots of campaigns have their piece of luck, but as the saying goes, "luck is what happens when preparation meets opportunity." That quote has become more famous than its alleged author, legendary football coach Darrell Royal.

It saves a lot of time when the cart stays in its proper place—behind the horse. The chapters and exercises in this workbook are designed to guide the capital campaign novice, and maybe some experienced folks too, through efficiently sequenced groups of preparatory steps. Steps within a group may occur together or in a different sequence, but the steps for each chapter are usually best taken in the order presented.

The benefits of a completed, successful campaign are many and glorious. In addition to the immense satisfaction of seeing your big ideas take shape, thanks to your new assets, you may see

- A more energetic, more unified, more knowledgeable, more effective board of directors

- A universally heightened appreciation among your donors and other constituencies for the special importance of your organization

- The translation of a new appreciation for your organization and the emotional highs from the campaign victory into (1) increased giving for ongoing needs and (2) increased numbers of people making both unrestricted and restricted program gifts

- An effective long-range plan

The development office stands to gain in a number of areas:

- Better connections to the organization and opportunities of interest to donors

- An improved ability to communicate with and attend to the needs of donors

- Better internal organization, hence, higher levels of productivity

- The ability to run minor campaigns in-house—the long-term pay-off for having a trained staff working with a well-honed organization

Sound interesting? Let's get started!

What Is a Capital Campaign?

Forms of Capital Campaigns

Examples of Capital Projects

The Stages of a Campaign

Do You Really Need a Capital Campaign?

When Should Your Organization Undertake a Capital Campaign?

What's in a Goal?

Does Your Organization Cope Well with Risk?

Understanding the Capital Campaign

IF YOU HAVE NEVER been through a capital campaign, this chapter will give you a quick overview and get you ready for the exercises in the following chapters.

What Is a Capital Campaign?

A capital campaign seeks "to raise a specified sum of money within a defined time period to meet the varied asset-building needs of the organization" (Rosso, 1991, p. 80). A campaign draws on all of an organization's strengths in pursuit of a fund raising goal. Driving the campaign are enthusiastic leaders, both volunteer and executive. The leaders inspire an established, loyal donor base to make exceptional gifts. The prospect base contains a sufficient number of people both able and willing to make the gifts you will need. A typical campaign endeavors to obtain commitments for a sum that can be from four to ten times the level of annual receipts. Put another way, if you were to spread all campaign commitments across the years of soliciting and collecting, you would need to be doubling or tripling your usual annual intake every year for five or six years. Campaigns are not for the faint of heart! But with proper preparation and leadership, you can indeed succeed.

Forms of Capital Campaigns

Four different campaign models are in common use, each having evolved to respond to differing types of organizations and circumstances. (For a fuller discussion of the models presented here, see Dove, 2000, pp. 16–19.)

1. *Historical campaign*—meets the organization's capital needs. You could seek funds for

    Building only

    Endowment only

    Combined building and endowment (popular for ensuring maintenance support for expanded space or programs)

2. *Comprehensive campaign*—combines under one, big umbrella current operations, one-time goals, and endowment objectives.

3. *Single-purpose campaign*—seeks funds for a specific purpose, usually with appeal to a special-interest constituency. This form is widely used in large, administratively complex organizations.

4. *Continuing major gifts program*—multiyear, staff-led subcampaigns that are smoothly integrated into the ongoing development program. This form of "perpetual campaigning" works well to further the clearly defined institutional goals.

Examples of Capital Projects

Here are examples of capital projects around which campaigns may be organized:

Building

New construction

Rehabilitation of old buildings

Land purchase

Landscaping

Renovation

Moving and space adaptation

Roof replacement

Endowment

Permanent fund (general or special purpose funds)

Endowed chairs or positions

Start-up funds for program expansion

Scholarship fund

Equipment purchase fund

The Stages of a Campaign

Generally, successful campaigns track the following five phases:

1. *Assessment and preparation* (one to four or more years)

2. *Organization and planning* (six months to one year)

3. *Quiet phase*—portion of the campaign that seeks first-tier (lead) gifts, second-tier (major) gifts, and third-tier (special) gifts (one to two or more years)

4. *Public phase*—balance of the campaign, seeking lower-level (general) gifts as well as all higher-level gifts (one to two years)

5. *Conclusion and pledge pay-out*—formal end of the campaign, continuation of solicitations of cultivated prospects, and collection of pledges (up to three more years)

A campaign could be as short as three years to prepare and complete or as long as ten.

Do You Really Need a Capital Campaign?

You know you have pressing needs on behalf of the people you serve, but is a capital campaign really the right fund raising vehicle for you?

➤ Assess Your Needs
(Part A)

If you feel compelled to answer yes to *any* of the questions in the following lists, read further. If your responses are not resoundingly positive, you might consider designing another approach, such as using a single-purpose fund within the context of your major-gift fund raising for ongoing operations and programs.

Do you truly *need* any of the following? That is, does your mission depend on it? Will your organization soar because of it? Check the appropriate box:

	Yes	Not Urgent
A new building or buildings	☐	☐
Renovations to a new building or buildings	☐	☐
Purchase of land or improvement of a building or buildings	☐	☐
A renovation or enlargement of your current site	☐	☐
A site furnished and equipped for programs	☐	☐
An endowment fund or additions to an endowment fund	☐	☐
Any other compelling need	☐	☐

Next, assess your real opportunities. Has an extraordinary opportunity come your way? Check the appropriate box:

	Yes	Possibly
Do you think your organization could advance to a new level?	☐	☐
Could a fund raising drive now ultimately yield a higher level of giving to your ongoing needs?	☐	☐
Is your organization a start-up looking to the community for facilities and significant start-up capital?	☐	☐

Assess Your Funding Sources (Part B)

If you had any yes responses, it is time to make a quick assessment of your funding sources.

Do you have donors or funders who could and might make an early gift to a campaign of 10 to 20 percent of a proposed goal?   Yes_____ No_____
Can you list three?

_____

_____

_____

At 5 percent of a proposed goal?   Yes_____ No_____
Can you list five?

_____

_____

_____

_____

_____

Do you have known prospects for major gifts to a campaign who are not donors now? (Foundations may fall into this category. Could your project be funded entirely by foundation or public funds? If so, you do not need a campaign; you need a lot of good, old-fashioned proposal development and follow-through.)

Yes_____ No_____

Can you list five?

_____

_____

_____

_____

_____

Assessing Whether to Investigate a Capital Campaign (Part C)

If you had at least one yes answer from Part A and at least two names for each question in Part B, by all means continue to investigate a capital campaign.

If you were stumped by the questions in Part B, you should probably shift your focus to building up a major gifts program first.

When Should Your Organization Undertake a Capital Campaign?

The best answer is this: when you are ready. In the real world, however, timing sometimes compels a campaign before all the elements are in place, particularly when a hurricane, flood, or earthquake threatens or has already done its worst. By working through this book, you will learn where you fall short and where to put your focus to catch up or minimize your weaknesses and still be ready enough for success.

Organizations sometimes undertake a campaign "because we have no choice. We must do this now." Or the need appears so pressing that "we are doing this no matter what anybody says." Just be aware of the risks. Inadequately prepared campaigns launched with the imperative of great urgency—even with their inherent appeal—can stall, and stall soon.

Good judgment, born of experience, can help you decide whether you are "ready enough." That is one of the key roles played by consultants. The hard truth of the matter is that unless you have an angel on your shoulder, there are no shortcuts. The outsized nature of a campaign brings great new stresses on an organization. Granted, the very exercises for getting ready can be stressful, but the good news is that they condition the entire organization's strength and ability to chart a future.

A decision on timing your campaign undertaking—deciding when to launch—must take into consideration your organization's preparedness concerning a large number of variables. Ultimately, the decision to move ahead must proceed from the good judgment of your trustees, your executive staff, and your consultant, should you engage one.

There are three levels to readiness. We'll walk through each one.

1. *Institutional readiness.* You have a strong, clear rationale for your programs. You have a strong history of accomplishment and a good reputation. You have well-developed giving programs. Planning is well managed; you have developed a thorough strategic plan. Other plans you need are in hand or under way. (See "Preparing Your Institutional Plan" in Chapter Two for descriptions.) You have capable, committed leadership; volunteer leadership is in place, experienced, and knowledgeable about fund raising. Staff executive leadership is in place, experienced, and knowledgeable about fund raising as well as management. Your organization is staffed with people who do their jobs well.

2. *Project readiness.* You have done your homework on your choices and what the best options will require. The solution you have chosen is defensible and compelling.

3. *Market readiness.* You have evidence that a sufficient number of your leading donor prospects like the vision and the project and stand ready to assist.

IMPORTANT CAMPAIGN SKILLS AND KNOWLEDGE

The following are some of the types of skills and knowledge that your organization will need in order to conduct a successful campaign:

Verbal and Presentation Skills

- Strong writing skill, to bring out a compelling case for both the institution and its capital needs
- Speaking and group presentation skills

Analytical and Institutional Skills

- Understanding of strategic analysis
- Knowledge of organizational and tactical planning

Financial Knowledge

- How to budget and do multiyear forecasting
- How to use borrowing as a strategy
- How to assess an organization's capacity to borrow and carry a loan
- How to work with a lender
- How to investigate bond issues and other types of government subventions

Fund Raising Skills

- Knowledge of how to develop contributed and grant income resources
- Knowledge of record-keeping systems and procedural skills
- General understanding of planned giving

Human Resources Knowledge

- Knowledge of how to develop professional human resources
- Knowledge of team management
- An understanding of individual behavior in both volunteer and professional settings
- An understanding of group behavior in both volunteer and professional settings

Marketing and Communications Skills

- Knowledge of how to develop marketing concepts
- Knowledge of how to communicate various types of information via various types of media to various groups of people

Project Management Skills

- How to select the right group of people for a facility project team
- How to translate program needs into physical space and facility needs
- How to select an architect
- How to work with an architect and read plans
- How to develop a comprehensive project budget
- How to maintain control of project costs

A development director needs to know the following:

- What motivates people to give major gifts
- How to help the organization always to make the best impression
- How to create and use persuasive tools and techniques
- How to organize and clearly present complex information
- How to tell a compelling story with both narrative and numbers (text and images, budgets and financial projections)
- How to manage proper communications with all donor constituencies
- How to build teams with a wide variety of people
- How to find effective ways to approach problems
- Tact and sensitivity in handling donor interests and personal information
- How to keep spirits up

What's in a Goal?

It is a common myth that the campaign goal equals the construction costs. In fact, there are up to five distinct classes of costs related to capital projects; construction and fund raising are just two of them. It is extremely important that all five be understood separately and budgeted for accordingly.

1. Institutional Planning

The institutional plan has two layers. The *strategic plan* (three to five years) presents an overall rationale and vision (sometimes labeled "goals"). It shows how general goals (sometimes termed "objectives") will help realize the vision. (For details, see Bryson and Alston, 1995.)

The *tactical and business plans* show specific activities two to three years out, but they project expenses and income figures to one year beyond the completion of your project, when all associated new costs will have been triggered. These plans specify activities that will achieve objectives and goals for program, governance, and revenue generation.

It costs a lot of time, effort, and money to prepare a comprehensive institutional plan. However, since most funders now view planning as an ordinary demonstration of good governance and ongoing management, not a special case, most institutions would be well advised to budget for planning as an annual expense. You may find in your case, however, that it is useful to group these kinds of costs in a capital start-up budget.

2. Project Planning

Project planning includes *physical assessment* and *design management*. If your campaign will be for plant and equipment costs, you will need to budget adequate advance funds for space analysis and planning, equipment needs analysis, architectural design, and related tasks.

This plan maps the route through all the concrete steps of assembling groups to determine the exact nature and scope of the project, its site, its requirements, selection of architects and builders, the project's development, its construction management, its financial management, and its proper execution.

3. Facilities Planning

A *facilities plan,* when needed, translates agreed-on program needs and objectives from the institutional plan into square footage and physical space arrangements. The facilities plan should also address building systems and telecommunications.

4. Project and Construction Costs

The budget you negotiate with the builder is just one factor in determining your *total costs for construction*. In addition, you will need to tally the expenses you incur on account of the construction. Such items can include loss of attendance and earned revenue, loss of interest income, new interest payments on loans, temporary relocation costs, and long-term storage. (You will be asked to fill in the numbers for such a project budget in Chapter Three).

5. Campaign Costs

Campaign costs are the costs directly related to bringing in funds, including executive and support staffing—the greatest expenses—consultants' fees, public relations materials and marketing collateral, communications, office and equipment expenses, pledge attrition (people who pledge but don't pay), and prospect cultivation expenses. According to statistics compiled by the National Society of Fund Raising Executives, most campaign costs average between 5 and 15 percent of the funding goal.

It should not surprise you to learn that the percentage of costs per dollar raised tends to decrease as the goal increases. Staffing costs per gift solicited are fairly constant, so the ability to attract larger gifts and greater numbers of effective volunteer solicitors drops the cost per gift. (See the Resources section for more detail.)

Generally speaking, the smaller campaigns (up to $5 million) may cost at least 15 percent of the goal. Larger campaigns ($25 million and up) could cost under 10 percent of the goal.

Does Your Organization Cope Well with Risk?

Any major undertaking into uncharted territory carries risk, and campaigns are certainly no exception. The good news is that most of the risks can be anticipated and prepared for. But scarcely any campaign escapes without at least one unexpected turn or even roadblock.

How risk-friendly is your organization? If you believe your board or staff could not weather the common experiences listed next, it may be the wiser course to delay a campaign.

Risk-Assessment Quiz

Try ranking each of these potential scenarios on a risk-friendly scale of 1 to 5. A rank of 1 means "Entirely too scary; we would not move ahead." A rank of 5 means "We would plunge in anyway!"
Code: 1 = Turn back; 5 = Bring it on!

_____ The annual fund could dip 10 percent or more when some donors prefer to designate all their giving to the campaign.

_____ Campaign leadership could be too slow to come together, stalling the campaign before it gets started.

_____ The campaign chair(s) might suddenly step down.

_____ The CEO or executive director might leave mid-campaign.

_____ The development director might leave mid-campaign.

_____ The economic climate for giving could take a tumble, throwing all the forecasts off.

_____ A mainstay source of funds to the annual budget could begin to shrink or become unreliable.

_____ Primary funders or donors with whom you have been negotiating all along might change or get new mandates or need to delay matters.

_____ Your Total Score

If you scored less than 25, your organization may need further preparation. Excessive fear can foster early burnout and damaging turnover. A score of 25 or higher indicates that your organization could likely weather the occasional turbulence in a campaign and persevere. So if you're game, let's get ready!

THE FIVE MOST COMMON MYTHS ABOUT A CAPITAL CAMPAIGN

The Nonprofit Finance Fund provides capital loans to nonprofit groups, along with excellent technical workshops on how to plan for capital projects and their associated campaigns. They often begin their workshops by debunking these all-too-common myths:

- Fund raising can be delegated to the staff.
- Fund raising can be delegated to the board.
- Fund raising can be delegated to a consultant.

- Capital campaigns come to an end. (Actually, prospects keep surfacing, and the process of converting them to donors is a lengthy one; needs and opportunities keep appearing.)

- The campaign goal equals the construction costs. Many types of costs will need to be covered. See "Cost Categories for the Bricks-and-Mortar Capital Campaign" on pages 71–73 for a list of costs to budget.

WHY PROPER PLANNING IS CRITICAL TO SUCCESS

Campaigns launched without proper preparation run a serious risk of falling short or stalling.

Failing to meet the goal can place many burdens on you. Here are some of the big ones. You might

- Add an expensive new element to annual financial obligations that seriously debilitate needed program services.

- Demoralize leadership; important volunteers may leave the organization, along with their financial commitments.

- Damage credibility in the community, making fund raising for ongoing operations all the more difficult and new volunteers all the more difficult to recruit.

- Contribute to a higher level of staff turnover, further impeding the delivery of high-quality services.

Stalling must also be taken seriously. A long stall can damage an institution. Here are few reasons why:

- Funds may stop arriving while costs continue.

- Campaign volunteer leadership may leave.

- Key staff may leave.

- Conditions affecting the campaign may change so much during the lull that you may need to fund many preparation and start-up costs all over again.

- You may lose credibility, which would affect everything from annual fund raising to board recruitment to staff recruitment, to say nothing of your ability to attract major, campaign-level gifts.

- Your costs may outrun your estimates to such an extent that you are unable to complete the work. You risk either disappointing donors or having grants rescinded or both.

Telling Your Story

Putting Strong Volunteer Leadership in Place

Evaluating Your Donor and Prospect Base

Preparing Your Institutional Plan

Getting Professional Support in Place

Establishing Effective Communications Channels

Establishing Visibility

Paying for Building Your Organization's Capacity

Getting the Organization Ready

INDIVIDUALS DO NOT raise money by themselves; individuals raise money on behalf of reputable organizations. Only when the organization is delivering needed or wanted services in an efficient and desired manner—and when this can be compellingly demonstrated—can people raise major funds on the organization's behalf.

A campaign is so much larger than business as usual that it puts everything to the test. The organization must be strong. All management systems must be sound enough to carry the strain. Governance by the board must be developed and in good working order. The vision must be well articulated and universally shared. Executive leadership must be in place, experienced, able, and trusted. Adequate staff support must be in place. Communication must be reliable and trusted. The organization must be well regarded already by those whom you would engage in a campaign.

But what, specifically, does your organization need to have in place to support a capital campaign? First, you need to get the word out.

Telling Your Story

The main reason your prospects will give is that they are moved to care. Begin to assemble your most compelling story. Build the outlines that will make it easily clear to readers and viewers just who will gain from your organization's work and how that will happen. This is source work for later use.

How to Tell Your Story

Begin by collecting the following:

Highlights of Your Services and Your History

Whom have you helped in the past?

Is highlight information already prepared?

If not, who will write or update it?

Compelling Narratives

List your best three stories.

1.

2.

3.

Are they well told?

Where?

List your best three story prospects (not yet told).

1.

2.

3.

Who will collect these?

When?

Images (Photographs, Drawings, Sketches)

Find and list two of your most arresting *images of people.*

1.

2.

Find and list two of your compelling images of the *results* of your work.

1.

2.

List three ideas for collecting strong, updated images.

1.

2.

3.

Who will get them?

Testimonials

Collect at least fifteen quotes from those who have been helped by your programs, as well as from those who have done the helping—both workers and donors. Attach them here.

Putting Strong Volunteer Leadership in Place

You must begin early to identify your volunteer leadership. A campaign sinks or swims on the strength of its volunteer leadership. Period.

Leadership stands firmly, however, *only* when the professional leadership of the institution is in place and has been working well with existing volunteer leaders.

Is yours an informed, committed board of directors? Do board members contribute their time *and* money to support the cause? Do board leaders (officers, committee chairs) make gifts in a timely way? If not, they will not be able to ask others to make gifts.

Here are some questions to help the board prepare:

➤ Board Readiness Quiz

To begin assessing your board's readiness, fill in the blanks:

What percentage of the board makes an annual gift?

If the percentage is low (under 80 percent), what do you estimate the likelihood to be of getting the levels of giving up to 90 or 100 percent (the figure more and more donors and grantors want to see)?

_____Low   _____Moderate   _____High

If board participation is too low to support the intensity of a campaign, what are the chances in the near future of bringing on new board members who can and will support a campaign?

_____Low   _____Moderate   _____High

If the board of directors has not and probably will not assume responsibility for fund raising, is there an auxiliary group who *can* take over the campaign leadership roles?

_____Yes   _____No   _____Maybe

If none exists, could one be created?   _____Yes   _____No   _____Maybe

Is the board united in its thinking?_____

Will every member of the board commit to working on a campaign in some capacity?

_____Yes   _____No   _____Maybe

Does your board membership list at least ten members who can give and get contributions?

_____Yes   _____No

You will need "High" or "Yes" answers to all these questions if you are to proceed with safety and assurance.

Leadership of the Board

Does your board as a whole have business-minded leadership and management? These traits will give a board the advantage when preparing for and carrying through a campaign. How close does your current board come? You can also apply the checklist that follows to new candidates for board membership (along with other criteria) to ensure that you are building the right kinds of strengths.

▶ Is Your Board Business–Minded?

In the quiz to follow, check all items for which you are comfortable that the answer is yes.

Does your board have

_____The ability to assess and undertake risk?

_____A commitment to oversight of standard business controls and financial management policies?

_____A marketing perspective, that is, a willingness to invest in communications programs that study and incorporate a donor's or participant's point of view and needs?

_____A commitment to attainment of professional management and supervisory skills for staff?

_____A commitment to appropriate levels of equipment and systems support?

_____A commitment to a culture of thanks and acknowledgment for both staff and volunteers?

_____The ability to sustain optimism and cheer others on?

When you can check all items, you have a board that will back sound preparation for a campaign.

What helps increase board participation and understanding? The following are most important:

Leadership from the chair of the board. The chair makes her or his own gifts first, is willing to solicit other board members, and is willing to call or write board members to hold them to their pledges.

Good communications. Hold regular one-on-one meetings between the executive director, CDO (chief development officer), program directors (faculty, department directors), and board members. Note that

- Timely communication and access to board members by key staff is essential.

- The CDO should be comfortable talking with *all* board members about their volunteer jobs.

- Simple cost-benefit analyses should be prepared wherever possible to gain support for key investments.

- Comparables should be provided, that is, benefits to other organizations when they made similar investments.

Satisfying committee work. Assign clear jobs for board members to do. Designate milestones and celebrate accomplishments.

Shared vision. The following tips can help ensure that board members do share a vision and a commitment.

- Gain clear agreement by the board about the direction of the organization, and confirm their mutual commitment.

- Hold board retreats on the issues and future of the organization and the role of the board in leading the organization.

- Engage facilitators who are experts in board development, governance, and board fund raising roles.

Feeling appreciated. Handle board members' gifts of time, talent, and treasure in respectful and thoughtful ways. You should

- Give members consistent, courteous treatment.

- Offer timely thank-you's for all efforts. Staff should also thank all board members. The board chair and committee chairs should find ways to thank other board members.

To start the ball rolling:

- Do your best to learn about and understand the fundamentals of good management.

- Do your best to a support a culture of thanks and acknowledgment.

- Keep your own spirits high and urge others on.

- Learn about group dynamics. Do not rely on group meetings to introduce proposals or evaluations. Meet one-on-one first with the leaders who can introduce or advance ideas and proposals at the committee or board level.

- Read up on personal incentives. What personal rewards matter to your constituents? Research their effectiveness and build them into your programs.

Role of the Development Committee of the Board

Your current development committee will have a key role to play at this stage and during the campaign. As the overall giving policy group, this committee recommends the general policies of the campaign to the full board. The actual work may be delegated to a campaign steering committee.

The development committee generally oversees overall operation of the campaign, including staffing and budget requirements.

The committee acts to prepare the campaign by ensuring the development of policies for the following:

- The campaign goal and its relationship to the annual campaign goal

- The campaign time line

- The kinds of gifts that may and may not be accepted (for example, real estate or certain types of in-kind donations)

- Guidelines under which memorial gifts or named gift opportunities may be established

- Gifts offered with unacceptable restrictions

- Gift acknowledgment and donor recognition programs

During the campaign, the development committee should serve as a liaison to the campaign leadership committee. At least one development committee member should sit on the leadership committee as a liaison to the board of directors.

A staff professional coordinates the development committee. When campaign counsel is hired, counsel should attend meetings when there is campaign business to be discussed.

Role of the Board of Directors in the Campaign

All board members need to participate in the campaign, demonstrating leadership by

- Making a stretch gift to the campaign

- Being available by telephone for occasional consultation

- Advising on prospect names, request levels, and timing of solicitations as requested

- Searching for new prospects

- Participating in cultivation events (together with other members of the board)

- Taking on specific assignments to ask for gifts

Leadership of the Campaign Steering Committee

Now it's time to begin shaping your campaign planning steering committee. This is the primary internal group that will focus on the steps through preparation and planning. In the campaign, it may become the leadership committee, adding members to lead solicitation efforts. The leadership exercises on the next pages may be worked through at the staff level first, but they should be repeated with the following group members in an assessment work session.

- Executive director
- Chair of the board
- Chair of board development (or advancement) committee
- Chair of board strategic planning committee
- Other key board member(s)
- Chief development (advancement) officer

Next, look within your own ranks for volunteers who, you believe, can and would be willing to work toward and perhaps lead a campaign. Remember, you are not asking them to serve yet!

WHAT TO LOOK FOR IN YOUR LEADERSHIP

1. People with capacity at or over the top of your scale.
2. Willingness to give to your cause.
3. Willingness to solicit others.
4. People with access to wealth.

5. People with leadership skills and charm (so useful!).
6. People with enough time for meetings, reading reports, calls, and visits.
7. People who will do what they commit to do.

Potential Campaign Candidates

Can you name candidates for the following campaign positions?

- *Campaign chair or cochairs.* Campaign leaders provide the core of your campaign engine. Without proper leadership, your campaign will suffer great difficulty. It is worth your time to find the individual or individuals who will be able to provide the care and effort your campaign will need. Seek active leaders who will assemble and inspire other volunteers, expect accountability for campaign assignments, and lead by the example of their own generous gifts. The ideal chair will make a lead gift equal to 10 to 20 percent of the goal. List three candidates:

1. _____

2. _____

3. _____

- *Honorary chair or cochairs.* Symbolic leaders who will serve as ambassadors of the campaign from time to time and set the pace by the example of their own lead gifts. List three candidates:

1. _____

2. _____

3. _____

- *Key committee chairs.* You'll want your committee chairs to have strengths in all these areas:

  Access to wealthy individuals
  Access to corporate CEOs
  Access to individuals who give through or are influential with private foundations
  Access to legislators and a willingness to work with legislators
  Board members who can help you find or rate (decide how much to request from) your best prospects

List six candidates:

1. _____

2. _____

3. _____

4. _____

5. _____

6. _____

Constitute the steering committee from your lists. Select a chair from the board of directors. At least one other member should also sit on the development committee. Invite up to six or so of your other good prospects to join the steering committee. Too large a group can make planning a slow process.

What if you don't see enough strong volunteer leaders on your lists? Here are recruiting steps you can take:

- Follow stepwise practices to build board membership (see page 29).

- Activate committees and strengthen committee work.

- Ask board leaders to host informational receptions to which new prospects are invited.

- Invite key members from the community to take part in substantive brainstorming and planning sessions.

SAMPLE JOB DESCRIPTIONS FOR VOLUNTEER LEADERSHIP
Campaign Leadership Committee (Campaign Cabinet)

The leadership committee provides general direction and active oversight of the program. Confidentiality and anonymity are absolutely essential to this committee.

Honorary Cochair

Honorary cochairs help encourage campaign prospects to join their vision for the campaign's goals in light of their endorsement and lead gifts to the campaign. Cochairs may also help with targeted solicitations in certain instances.

Campaign Cochair

This person provides overall vision to the campaign and is a symbol of the commitment needed to achieve the goal. Cochairs solicit or help solicit strategic gifts. They may also chair meetings of the leadership committee. Top campaign leadership is accountable to the chair for meeting their commitments.

All Members

All members participate in the campaign by

- Making a stretch gift (This is essential! The ability to influence others to make major gifts depends on the demonstration of one's own personal philanthropy.)

- Attending one meeting per month at the outset (Frequency may change with time and season.)

- Being available by telephone for occasional consultation

- Reviewing prospect names, request levels, and timing of requests

- Searching for new prospects

- Participating in cultivation events

- Asking for gifts (Asks are made in teams or singly when appropriate; special sessions will orient leadership members to this process. Volunteers should carry only a small group of prospects at any one time.)

All members advise on policies and activities. Some examples are

- Gift acceptance policies

- Gift acknowledgment and recognition ideas and policies (naming opportunities, special invitations, donor wall display, and so on)

- Cultivation time line

- A communications plan (committee communications, donor communications)

All members advise on materials for use in the campaign. Examples are

- Campaign name and logo

- Strength of the case for the financial need and scenario

- Strength of the case for the program or mission benefit brought by the [object of your campaign]

- Strength of the case for the fit of the campaign with the Institutional Plan

- Representation of the case in a brochure

All members help make donors feel great by

- Telephoning or jotting short thank-you notes to assigned prospects who have made gifts

- Saying thanks to donors when they see them in person

All members enjoy driving this great cause by

- Enjoying time on-site with friends

- Accepting heartfelt thanks for their important work

Evaluating Your Donor and Prospect Base

"Do the work to prospect for the very large gifts that are so essential," Hank Rosso advised. Do you have a history of gift support? It is difficult indeed embarking on a campaign when your organization has had little or no experience developing and tending donors. Start-ups have little choice and must build as they go, but it is necessarily slow going. Before you jump into a campaign, let's take a look at your organization's experience.

➤ Your Record of Giving

Do you have a consistent record of giving over the last three years from the sources you are most likely to solicit for your campaign? "Yes" answers are what you need.

Individuals?	Yes_____	No_____	Somewhat_____
Foundations?	Yes_____	No_____	Somewhat_____
Corporations?	Yes_____	No_____	Somewhat_____
Public funds?	Yes_____	No_____	Somewhat_____

Have you had a major gifts program in place for at least two years? A major gift is one large enough that you have decided it deserves a personal mission to secure it. However, the visit to secure a gift is more about the donor than the gift. First become friends and establish emotional connections; then gifts will come. Thus the face-to-face visit forms the centerpiece of major gifts programs.

If you do have a major gifts program in place, it is well worth reviewing what works well and what could use some tuning.

➤ Strengths and Challenges

Please note these questions for future use:

What are the three biggest *strengths* of your major gifts program?

1. _____
2. _____
3. _____

What are the three biggest *challenges* of your major gifts program?

1. _____
2. _____
3. _____

RELATIONSHIPS THAT CAN HELP BUILD MAJOR GIFTS PROGRAMS

The chief executive plays a central role in a capital campaign. Campaign staff cannot succeed without her or him. The chart below shows the proper focus of the executive and shows which members of the staff carry the day-to-day responsibility for a given source of funding.

Source	Relationship	Strategy	Comments
Individuals	Director to individuals Board to individuals Staff maintains	Personal fit Best delivery and access	Director needs to devote much time to this.
Government	Staff to staff	Project or program fit Staff-driven	
Foundations	Staff to staff Board to foundation staff Board to foundation trustees	Project match Relevance to long-term goals (yours or theirs)	Director-level involvement is important or key for large grants.
Board	Staff maintains Board to individuals Director to individuals	Personal fit Director-driven	Director needs to devote much time to this.
Business	Staff to staff Board to executives	Program match Marketing match Peer match Staff-driven	From time to time needs presence of the director.

Note: Donors and prospective donors nearly always need to talk with the chief executive about an organization's vision and plans before making a major gift.

What if you do not have a strong board or a major gifts program in place? You will need to spend some time with the basics of board building and institutional development. If you are unsure whether these building blocks are really strong enough, or if you need to know how to build them, you might call for an outside institutional or development audit.

The term *audit* here has nothing to do with financial statements. What it does have in common with financial audits is that it's a rigorous, thorough evaluation of an organization's infrastructure. In order to gain a better perspective on the ability to raise funds (long before a major fund raising project is needed), organizations sometimes ask for an outside consultant to conduct an assessment and recommend a plan. The development audit will review strengths and weaknesses as they pertain to an agency's potential to raise funds and grow. Much of the content of such a study may resemble parts of the campaign feasibility study (see Chapter Four). Organizations looking ahead to a capital campaign may benefit from the multi-year course of preparation such a study can recommend.

TWELVE STEPS TO RECRUITING EFFECTIVE BOARD MEMBERS

Following clear steps can help you add wonderful new people to your board. Be sure to pack properly for the trip, however. You will need agreements on the board's governing purpose (clear by-laws), as well as on individual and committee responsibilities and jobs. A chart of committees and their structure should be in place or part of an articulated institutional plan.

1. Identify your criteria for new board members and prioritize them.

2. Identify prospects for new board members.

3. Identify contact people to link you to prospects for new board members.

4. Introduce prospects to your organization.

5. Invite prospects on a site visit and ensure a successful experience.

6. Identify and assess the prospects' interest, fit, needs, and so forth.

7. Repeat steps 5 and 6 until it is clear that you have a match. If you have an advisory or other

"friends" group, invite the prospects to join that group.

8. Now the nominating committee recommends to the board of directors that the prospect be invited to join the board.

9. The board votes to accept the nominating committee's recommendations.

10. Invite the prospect to join the board; provide full disclosure of obligations and opportunities.

11. Hold an orientation for new board members.

12. Finally, the board chair and the committee heads invite new members onto appropriate board committees.

IDENTIFYING AND RECRUITING CAMPAIGN LEADERS

Campaign leaders provide the core of your campaign engine. Without proper leadership, your campaign will suffer great difficulty, at a minimum. It is worth your time and care to locate people who will be able to provide the time and care your campaign will need.

What do you ask for? Look for the maximum:

- A lead gift
- Commitment to seeking out and asking others for major gifts

- Willingness to act as a visible ambassador on behalf of the campaign
- Commitment to inspire and set deadlines for the rest of the campaign team

But be realistic. Overloading a chair can derail a campaign; underloading a chair may mean the train scarcely leaves the station. You will need the ability to support your chosen leadership in appropriate and necessary ways. In recruiting, you will need to be concise, clear, and specific about roles and responsibilities for leadership as well as the use of their time.

Where does leadership come from? Most often these sources supply the leaders, in this order:

- Current board members
- Past board members
- Other key volunteers

- Community leaders
- Corporate and industry leaders

Now, we'll work through the following questions:

Do you have potential major gift contributors?

Do you have an established donor base?

If so, can you readily identify potential major gifts for a campaign from your donor lists?

How much would you need to raise from your donors to set your proposed campaign on its way?

There are two general ways to build campaigns: traditional and nontraditional. Let's look at how your donor base measures up in each case.

Traditional: The Pyramid Campaign Model

In a traditional capital campaign, the most capable, committed leaders set the pace by making lead-off gifts of an impressive size relative to the campaign goal. This act raises morale, spirit, and optimism. The size of a gift made by the chair or cochairs, relative to their ability to give, carries immense symbolic significance. It signals to the community what the project to be supported is truly "worth." The psychology is that others will then key their giving to the lead gift(s). The larger the lead gifts, the faster the campaign proceeds (provided you have enough prospects). There are many examples of donors making gifts greater than the chair's, but seldom will individuals stretch farther than they perceive the campaign leadership to have stretched. There is an efficiency to this top-down type of campaign that makes it the primary, enduring model.

To understand whether your donor base might be able to support a traditional campaign, you will need to draw up a trial "gift table" for the campaign goal you would like to set. A gift table is a time-tested way of sketching out your likelihood of succeeding. So let's build a traditional table. Your final figures may not match what we present, but this is a reasonable starting place. (In the larger campaigns, the top ten to fifteen gifts will account for 40 to 60 percent of the total. Smaller campaigns have a challenge to match that.)

Campaign Gift Table (Pyramid)

Proposed Campaign Goal: $_____

Number of Gifts Needed	Gift Range			Total Percentage	Number of Prospects Needed
1	10%–20% of goal	=	$_____	10%–20%	4–5
2	5%–10% of goal	=	$_____	15%	6–8
4	2.5% of goal	=	$_____	10%	16
8	1%+ of goal	=	$_____	10%	30
16	00.6% of goal	=	$_____	10%	50
32	00.3% of goal	=	$_____	10%	100
64	00.15% of goal	=	$_____	10%	200
A great many smaller gifts				5%–15%	
	_____			100%	

Traditional practice calls for identifying anywhere from three to four times the number of prospects you will need at each giving level to meet the odds of actually securing a gift at that level. So let's put some names to your top prospect levels and see how you stand.

First, here's a question everyone asks: Can I list prospects in more than one place? Yes, you can. But be careful; that's one reason you should quadruple your chances at any one level, especially the top levels, where each gift propels the campaign significantly.

Fill in the blanks that follow, first with names of individuals. List only those donors who have been giving to your organization long enough to have established strong connections. (New prospects usually need anywhere from eighteen months to two years of getting acquainted before they are ready to consider a major appeal.) Next, list foundations, bequests, and other planned gifts, bond measure prospects, and other special sources. You may also include allocations from your general fund activities that might help you reach your goal (net proceeds dedicated from an annual dinner, for example).

➤ Prospects for Funds

1 gift needed for 10%–20% of goal = $_____

    1. _____

    2. _____

    3. _____

    4. _____

    5. _____

2 gifts needed for 5% of goal = $_____

    1. _____

    2. _____

    3. _____

    4. _____

    5. _____

    6. _____

    7. _____

    8. _____

    9. _____

    10. _____

    11. _____

    12. _____

4 gifts needed for 2.5% of goal = $_____

    1. _____

    2. _____

    3. _____

    4. _____

    5. _____

    6. _____

    7. _____

    8. _____

    9. _____

    10. _____

    11. _____

    12. _____

    13. _____

    14. _____

15. _____

16. _____

8 gifts needed for 1.25% of goal = $_____

1. _____

2. _____

3. _____

4. _____

5. _____

6. _____

7. _____

8. _____

9. _____

10. _____

11. _____

12. _____

13. _____

14. _____

15. _____

16. _____

17. _____

18. _____

19. _____

20. _____

21. _____

22. _____

23. _____

24. _____

25. _____

26. _____

27. _____

28. _____

29. _____

30. _____

31. _____

32. _____

Continue your analysis with printouts from your database. Clearly, the more gifts you can obtain at the higher levels, the less work your campaign will entail.

Nontraditional: Multiple-Lead-Gifts Campaign Model

In a nontraditional campaign, there are no pace-setting mega-gifts. Many prospects of varying ability may be asked to make gifts at fixed, possibly symbolic, levels that together will add up. An example is a recent campaign run by a legal association in San Francisco on behalf of their volunteer services arm. The organization decided to celebrate a milestone anniversary with an endowment-plus campaign (also funding its move to new quarters). Lead gifts were sought from law firms only at a fixed level—the same for everyone. Lesser gifts followed (from lesser firms, went the psychology), and the campaign finished up with appeals to the individual membership. The campaign began with an initial goal of $1.5 million and concluded by exceeding an upwardly revised goal of $3 million.

Here is sample gift table for a campaign that would flatten the traditional pyramid into a trapezoid. (Very large campaigns, with goals of more than $100 million, may also substitute a 10 percent lead gift with multiple lead gifts at levels below 10 percent.)

Campaign Gift Table (Multiple-Lead-Gifts)

Campaign Proposed Goal: $___/___/___/___

Number of Gifts Needed	Gift Range	Total Percentage
12	2.5% of goal = $_____	30%
16	1.25% of goal = $_____	20%
24	00.6% of goal = $_____	15%
48	00.3% of goal = $_____	15%
67	00.15% of goal = $_____	10%
Many		10%
		100%

Do you have the prospects for such a campaign? List thirty prospects for your top giving level and forty prospects for the second, equaling 50 percent of your campaign goal. (Use your own paper or the end pages for this exercise, please.)

The Many-Small-Gifts Campaign Model

Every once in awhile, an organization tries to raise large sums of money the old-fashioned, grassroots way. Many years ago, a prominent national dance company tried to raise $1 million for an endowment fund via direct mail. The letter informed recipients that the company had sent letters to one million dance lovers all over the country asking for just $1 each. Who couldn't respond to such a reasonable appeal? I sent them $1. As it turned out, I was in the minority. They did not quite lose money on the attempt. But they did not build much of an endowment, either.

Today, direct mail is used primarily as an investment practice to acquire the names of potential supporters. Ticketed events are also used for community campaigns. These and other methods constitute a very slow way to raise large sums.

WHICH GIFT MODEL MAKES THE MOST SENSE FOR YOUR ORGANIZATION?

In most instances, a version of the traditional model is the one best suited to the distribution of wealthy prospects in an organization. The nontraditional model can work when you can demonstrate that (1) you truly have enough prospects to raise 50 percent of your goal from the top two tiers, and (2) you have the dynamic leadership in place to influence and solicit the lead prospects.

Profile Your Individual Donors

Do you have identifiable constituencies (donor groups with identifiable characteristics)? What groups are your donors likely to belong to? Examples of constituencies are your board of directors or trustees, your network of business executives, congregation members, association members, your donor membership list, proven donors to a similar cause, volunteer support groups, association members, and your vendors.

You already know how to research whether or not you fall within the guidelines of a private or corporate foundation: you look it up. But what about the *individuals* who give to you? Who are all these people who support your cause? And where can you go to find more of them? When you can profile who gives to you, you have a better chance of finding more like them, faster. In order to design the best possible marketing plan during your campaign, you'll want to have done this homework first.

So let's take a look at the people who already give you the largest gifts—the people most likely to make gifts to your campaign. Ask members of the board development committee to respond to these lists as well. Profile all your best prospects for individual gifts.

➤ Major Giver Profile

Which of these is most important to your primary supporters?

_____Spiritual fulfillment

_____Social standing

_____Being a civic player

_____The cause itself

_____Being recognized and rewarded by peers

_____Giving back

_____Honoring family traditions

_____Exploring new territory and creating new solutions

_____

_____

_____

What kind of people are they?

_____Need to be personally involved

_____Respond better to concepts

_____Single-issue people

_____Renaissance people

_____Party goers

_____Party-averse people

_____Social networkers

_____Business networkers

_____Parents

_____Childless couples

_____Readers

_____Nonreaders

_____What else?

_____

_____

_____

What activities do they enjoy?

_____Parties and receptions

_____Sporting events

_____Exercise or amateur sports

_____Working around the house

_____Gardening

_____Shopping

_____

_____

_____

How do they get their information?

_____Word of mouth

_____Television

_____On-line, e-mail, Internet

_____Radio drive time

_____Radio late night

_____Business press

_____Club and society speakers

_____Specialty magazines

_____Social press

_____Children's schools and parent networks

_____Alumni associations

_____

_____

_____

In what forums is credibility created and confirmed for them?

_____Friends and personal networks

_____Television

_____On-line, e-mail, Internet

_____Radio talk shows

_____Business colleagues

_____Business press

_____Professional clubs

_____General press

_____Social press

_____Specialty press

_____

_____

_____

How can you best get their attention when you need to?

_____Personalized mailings

_____Post card

_____E-mail

_____Telephone (telephone tree)

_____Newsletter

_____Advertising

_____

_____

_____

_____

Most organizations have never undertaken any type of formal survey to learn basic marketing essentials about their givers. If yours is one of these, now would be a good time to conduct one.

With the help of your board (your first and best resource for credibility), you can create a confidential market survey of your top five hundred to one thousand donors. Take your time to craft a questionnaire that is sensitive and gets the information you want. Ask one or two board members to help you put it together. Test it on your board first. Let them edit the survey, even as they respond to it.

Remember, every point of contact is a point of cultivation. Doing this right will serve two important purposes. It will (1) help you design effective marketing communications for donors and prospects and (2) impress people and help bring your best prospects one step closer to a major gift. Doing it wrong will waste resources and turn back the clock on your prospects.

How do you ensure that your own people respond? All response programs need elbow grease. That's a fact. You may devise your own distribution system, but here is one approach. Simply follow these six steps:

1. Mail a colorful postcard to each of your five hundred to one thousand prospects, advising them that a short survey is on the way; explain why it is important.

2. One week later, mail the survey in a self-addressed, stamped envelope of the same color. (Provide an e-mail alternative for those who are online.) State a deadline prominently.

3. One week later, mail a second postcard advising of the urgency of response and thanking people if they have already returned the survey.

4. For some individuals, set breakfast or lunch appointments at which one of your board members can interview the donor and possibly fill out the form. Or you might catch prospects at your own receptions and take a moment for the brief interview. Each interaction is a good opportunity to talk about your organization without attaching a solicitation.

5. Mail a report and thank-you note to all invited participants. Urge anyone who has not responded to do so immediately.

6. Keep the program as an ongoing, informal project. The public relations officer can provide annual updates.

There is little mystery about why so few organizations have taken the steps listed: they require staff time and money—resources that are sometimes difficult to invest when there are competing, immediate demands. Yet an investment in donor marketing and communications programs can reap great benefits. Use charts like those in Exhibits 2.2 and 2.4, appearing later in this chapter, to develop and compare your costs for a mail survey program.

A plan to develop a good prospect list involves (1) knowing your names and (2) getting more names.

Knowing Your Names

Here is one of your biggest and most critical homework projects. To go into a campaign with confidence, you must know many things about your donors and your prospects.

Your donor database must be able to record at a minimum the answers to these four key questions:

1. Why does a given donor care about the work your organization does more than the work of the gazillion other charitable and educational projects in the world?

2. Who are the persons most responsible for getting the donor involved with your organization and keeping the person interested?

3. What is the relative giving capacity of the donor or prospect? What is the person's net worth? What can you learn about how much the person gives to other causes? Is timing for a major gift an issue?

4. When and how often does the prospect come to see you?

   In addition, it is good to know the answers to these questions:

   How much enthusiasm do you think the person feels for your organization currently?

   Are there individuals on staff to whom the donor has a special connection?

   Is there anything else from the market profile list in the previous section?

   Here's what to look for in your lists:

- Past giving at a level that is significant for your organization.
- Repeat giving. (Look through your database for donors who have been giving consistently over the years.)
- Repeat giving from people who could be wealthy. (Cross-check repeat donors for their residential area by zip code or by other indicators of wealth that you might have about them.)
- Your existing network. Cross-check the names of loyal donors with contact names from your organization; consider whether your network is strong.

Setting Up a Screening Committee

Assemble a small preliminary donor screening committee. The purpose of this group is to review your current list of donors for the names of people most likely to give to the capital project and at what general levels. The single most efficient way of gauging what level of commitment people might bring to a campaign is to get their friends to talk about them. The single biggest caveat in such a plan is, "Any two people can give away a third person's money." So says Henry Goldstein, president and CEO of The Oram Group, Inc., a long-established consulting firm to philanthropic organizations. Do keep this caveat in mind when your group meets to fill out the blanks in the gift tables listed earlier.

Who from the leadership can and will help anchor a preliminary donor screening committee?

Conducting Screening Sessions

Screenings, also known as rating sessions, generally take one of three forms: open group, "silent," and individual. All forms may be used, and certainly so during the intensive period when you are planning the logistics of the campaign itself. As you are still in a preparatory, assessment mode, we suggest that open-group sessions will suffice at this stage. The procedure goes something like this:

- *Gather your lists.* Start by asking your board for lists of colleagues, friends, and relatives. Ask other volunteers as well. Assemble lists of donors from your database who meet the top three criteria: history of sizable gifts to your organization or similar interests, possible capacity, repeat giving. Assemble the giving lists in annual reports from related organizations.

- *Provide a relaxed setting.* You will want to provide a pleasant experience, even a social experience with food and beverages, but the true purpose of the meeting is all business.

- *Set a business tone.* Emphasize the importance of confidentiality. Outline the content of the lists to be shared.

- *Ask for short meetings.* Ask for no more than ninety minutes for each meeting.

- *Review short lists.* Present names to review in batches of twenty-five to fifty. Long lists are overwhelming and depressing. Instead of feeling, "Wow, look at all these potential supporters," people think, "I'll never get out of here." People can feel more of a sense of accomplishment if they work through groups. If possible, organize them from your sense of the highest potential to the lowest.

- *Prepare prospect charts.* Column heads on the charts should be labeled to receive the key information you are after. Meeting participants should have these lists in front of them as they work through each group of names. Mark all lists "Confidential."

Fields for information should include at least the following:

Name

Address

Gift history and last gift

Largest gift and purpose

Estimated capacity for giving

Estimated likely gift to your organization (A simple multiple of past giving may greatly underestimate what a donor may be willing to give to a campaign.)

Existing links to your organization

Known sympathies for your cause

Best person(s) to cultivate or solicit them

Notes about personal and professional background and connections

Notes about other volunteer involvement and nonprofit affiliations

Codes: A = Ready to make a major gift; B = Needs some cultivation before a solicitation; C = Cold prospect; begin to cultivate.

Such questions are necessary to start. As you move into a campaign, you will want to invest in more research on your prospects. When you have filled in the blanks adequately, you will have the background to develop two essential strategies for your prospects: (1) how to prepare the cultivation and (2) how to prepare and conduct the solicitation.

Preparing to Capture Data from the Meeting

Prepare alternate, efficient ways to capture the data from the conversations. People tend to talk very rapidly and to jump about between categories and names. To get the best out of your sessions, note-takers must keep up. Here are a few methods:

- *Use tape recorders.* Tape recorders can be alienating, and their small microphones do not pick audio up well. But if your group trusts you to destroy the tape, recorders can save you much trouble and catch information you can miss while writing.

- *Start with large writing spaces.* Large spaces in the charts or on blank sheets of paper are handy for the extra notes that won't fit on your chart.

- *Designate scribes.* Choose people who can write really fast (remember shorthand?).
- *Type or write on a portable computer.* Typing is an old stand-by, but if you want to avoid the clack of a computer keyboard, the personal message pads that record hand-writing as digital text are an excellent resource.
- *Distribute individual donor information.* Use a new page for each new prospect or donor for whom you have incomplete information. Volunteers can take these with them to fill out at their leisure or, more effectively, use as talking guides while a staff member fills them out in a follow-up meeting (writing rapidly). *Remember:* a prospect has the legal authority to see anything that an organization has written about them. Record all notes as though the prospect could view them.

Be sure to collect all lists at the end of the meeting. Lists should not leave with participants. Staff may need to devote as much as a day to collating, analyzing, and reporting the information gleaned from a ninety-minute rating session. Data should yield initial cultivation and solicitation strategies, with chief emphasis on prospects with the most capacity and best record of giving to and contact with your organization.

Getting More Names

Readers may be familiar with the term *six degrees of separation.* Roughly, this theory suggests that the entire population of the world is linked by a chain of no more than six acquaintances. If we apply the same theory to our own communities, we quickly discover that most of the people we would like to reach are probably no more than two or three acquaintances away. The efficiency of a network becomes apparent. Over time, every well-purposed organization can engage successive links in the acquaintance chain.

Here are a few common methods you can use to capture more names.

- *Method A:* Ask key volunteers and board members for contacts to any acquaintances or professional colleagues with a possible interest in your organization's work.
- *Method B:* Match your volunteers with names you provide. If you use this method, follow these steps:

Step 1: Identify key names of people who are members of your prospective donor constituencies. These are often called suspects—not yet prospects.

Step 2: Ask your board and other key volunteers if they know any of the names.

Step 3: Research the professional and social affiliations of your most likely suspects. Acquire lists of people connected via these affiliations.

Again, see if your board and volunteers are acquainted with any names. Explore any matches.

- *Method C:* Look for names in your own membership lists.
- *Method D:* Note all offers and sign-ups.

There are many creative ways to capture names and addresses. Here are two general methods:

- *Example A:* An organization sets up a table or booth in an area frequented by groups of people who may include individuals friendly to the cause. A sign-up page for informational mailing is provided; names and addresses are added to the database for further cultivation.
- *Example B:* Special offers lead an individual to the organization's Web site, where a name and address can be left to receive information.

Transferring Donor Friendships

How well do your staff and board leadership know your donors? The more points of connection a donor has to an organization's leadership, the greater your chances that the donor will connect you to others, as well as become a major gift contributor.

Organize many opportunities for your volunteer solicitors to introduce their friends and colleagues to executive staff and other board members. Here are two ways to engage new donors with your organization: (1) invite donors to on-site programs, receptions, parties, and special events, and (2) invite clearly interested new donors onto volunteer committees, task forces, or advisory councils.

List (on your own paper!) some volunteer opportunities with your organization that you think could appeal to a donor or major gift prospect.

Preparing Your Institutional Plan

The organization that enters today's capital campaign world without a fully considered institutional plan is asking for difficulties at sensitive times. Your supporters and prospects expect you to have answered the hard questions before you ask them to get involved. Programs must be reasonably conceived for the foreseeable future (three to five years) in the context of an established need and supported by a plausible business plan.

As early as possible, you should engage supporters, your board, and prospects in helping with the organization's planning. There is hardly a better way to cultivate knowledgeable leaders for your institution and campaign.

PLANS YOU WILL NEED

What plans will you need to have developed to get ready to begin your campaign? Optimally, you need to have at least five types of plans before you launch your campaign. Budget for them.

1. Institutional plan
2. Facilities plan or master plan
3. Capital project management plan
4. Communications plan
5. Campaign plan

1. Institutional Plan

The *strategic plan* (three to five years) presents the overall rationale and vision and shows how general goals will achieve the vision.

The *tactical and business plans* detail activities with costs and revenues for two to three years out. Properly, you must show expense and income figures to at least one year beyond project completion; by then, all associated new costs will have been triggered. Detail when activities will achieve objectives and goals for program and support, governance, and revenue generation.

2. Facilities Plan or Master Plan

The facilities plan will show how your activity needs can be met in physical space. The facilities plan should address space options, building systems, and support for equipment and telecommunications. A master plan gives a detailed view of long-term goals.

3. Capital Project Management Plan

Your management plan plots the route from assembling groups to assessing the nature and scope of the project, its options for location and its requirements, selection of architects and construction management, financial management, and its proper execution in general.

4. Communications Plan

As you begin the planning for a campaign, you should work out your means, methods, and forms of communication with and between all constituencies: staff, board of directors, volunteer leadership, other key volunteers, donors, prospects, political representatives, and so forth. Later, when you are in the start-up phase of your campaign, you can complete your plans for more widely distributed updates, bulletins, and other types of progress reports and volunteer recognition.

5. Campaign Plan

The campaign plan is developed in detail during the start-up phase of the campaign. It allows the leadership to do the following to drive and support the fund raising effort:

- Develop volunteer leadership and a leadership structure.
- Prepare the final case.
- Prepare volunteers to solicit donations.
- Identify prospects.
- Develop cultivation and tracking methods.
- Conduct milestone planning.
- Develop acknowledgment and recognition programs.
- Establish timing.

What is an institutional or long-range plan? A sound institutional plan includes the vision, goals, and objectives (the strategic plan), as well as the proposed tactics for fulfilling the objectives (the business plan). The full ramifications of your capital project—whether building or endowment—will need to be represented in the plan. Financial projections will demonstrate how your organization will balance its budget during the campaign and once the capital work is completed.

If you don't have an institutional plan, you may need to obtain up-front planning costs of the following types:

- Institutional planning: facilitator, planner, staff time

- Master planning: facilities consultants, land-use specialists, staff time

- Site research: realtor, staff time

You can get planning money from these sources:

- Your board of trustees

- Carefully saved general funds

- Planning grants from foundations or other private funders

- Loans—commercial and private

The document of your institutional plan must clearly communicate the *vision* for your organization, your *rationale* for everything you are doing and planning to do, and your *specific action plan* for reaching your goals. Your people's credentials and those of the organization that is to accomplish the work should also be well documented. It is the best evidence you can give a potential funder that you know where you are headed and have a good chance of getting there. Your institutional plan is the foundation on which you will build the rationale for your capital project, along with your plan for financial health during and beyond your campaign.

In your plan, you should set forth this specific information:

- *Your mission and vision.* You should describe clearly the purposes for which your institution or agency is organized, as well as the envisioned role and level of effectiveness of your organization in meeting the general need(s) you describe and the role of your organization relative to others working to meet the need.

- *Who you are.* State what your organization does. You need to establish the credibility of your organization to persevere and succeed.

- *The goals and objectives that will advance you toward your vision.* Included here are institutional goals and specific objectives that will support the goals.

- *The tactics that will advance the objectives.* You need to detail activities and a staffing plan that will support agreed-on objectives. Develop here the rationale for any proposed changes or additions to facilities or permanent funds and the rationale for proposed permanent funds.
- *The financial plan.* Plan for how you will balance your budget over the next few years and after the capital campaign is concluded. Express your options, strategies, and challenges in multiyear income-expense financial spreadsheets.

For information about strategic planning, see Bryson and Alston (1995). For help with building the financial model for your plan, look to your CFO or to a board member with financial planning skills. You may wish to engage a consultant.

The buy-in and commitment of staff and program volunteers to the institutional plan, including the campaign options, is crucial to success. A healthy future and a healthy campaign need the support of the entire team. The people who carry your organization day to day—those who bring your services to those you serve—need to share the vision and planning for the future.

Building Internal Support

Who are your key internal constituencies? (Carry forward to page 67.)

1. _____
2. _____
3. _____
4. _____
5. _____

To which planning committees can each constituency best contribute?

1. _____
2. _____
3. _____
4. _____
5. _____

Do your internal constituencies agree that the organization really needs the improvements that would be the subject of a campaign?   Yes_____   No_____   Sort of_____

How will you build consensus for the goals, objectives, and methods of your institutional plan? Write your steps in the space below:

Getting Professional Support in Place

Now is the time to get knowledgeable staff and adequate support in place.

➤ Rate Your Staffing Strength

Do you have the ability to support the campaign with knowledgeable staff? Is your fund raising staff experienced, able, and educated in development? Is your development staff seasoned? Does leadership possess at least five years of management responsibility?

Yes_____   You're in shape to analyze your strengths and weaknesses and to move ahead.

Not enough_____   Get training and support pronto.

No_____   Build a knowledgeable development staff before attempting any campaign.

Do you have good internal support structures for fund raising? Rank your strengths in each of these areas from 1 to 10 (10 is highest):

_____Annual campaign (a volunteer-led, time-delimited solicitation program to raise funds from individuals, businesses, and others)

_____Prospect research on individuals

_____Proposal and case development

_____Budgeting and forecasting

_____Donor appeals and renewals by letter

_____Liaison with volunteer groups, "Friends of . . ." groups, auxiliaries, and so on

_____Benefit events

_____Ability to resist burnout

_____Total Score

You will need a score of at least 40 to risk moving ahead toward a campaign.

Look at your answers to the staffing quiz, and then consider what technology upgrades or new staffing needs might be required to bring your staff to campaign readiness. On the chart that follows the technical quiz, you will see a place to list your staff and technology needs, estimate their expense, and add the total into the campaign budget that you will spend during the start-up phase of the campaign, if not before.

Rate Your Technical Capabilities

It is extremely important to have an efficient database and computer network in place.

Rank your strengths in each of these areas from 1 to 10 (10 is highest):

_____Your ability to enter, store, retrieve, and communicate data in multiple formats gives your volunteers and donors confidence to keep working and giving. Inability to produce good, timely records can seriously damage the growth of long-term donor relationships.

_____Can your database store and relate all the records (the number of files for all your donors and prospects) you will want to accumulate during the campaign?

_____Can you pull reports sorting for gifts and donors by size and date of gift, cumulative giving, zip code, affiliations, and so forth?

_____Does everyone engaged with the fund raising department have their own workstation, and is everyone networked to each other and to the database?

_____How easily can various people in the fund raising department access needed data and produce reports?

_____Is your provision for systems maintenance up to the task?

_____Do you have a system in place to record donations and other pertinent data in a timely way?

_____Total Score

If your score is less than 50, you need to upgrade your systems and, perhaps, training, or even add staff.

━━━━▶ Review Your Stewardship Protocols

Examine your stewardship protocols. How fast is your turnaround time for thank-you letters and other acknowledgments?

Telephone calls to donors: within ____ day(s). (Over one day is not wonderful.)
Written notes: within ____ days. (Over three days is not wonderful.)

Estimate New Support Costs

Now is the time to estimate new support costs. Look at your answers to the questions, and note on the chart below what new staffing or systems upgrades might be required to bring your staff to campaign readiness. Do a preliminary estimate. You must budget for it, or it will not happen. See Exhibit 3.1, page 73, lines 78 and 79.

━━━━▶ New and Allocated Campaign Staff and Support Costs

New Staff Position	Percentage Full-Time Equivalent	Salary Range	Totals
_____	_____	_____	_____
_____	_____	_____	_____
_____	_____	_____	_____
_____	_____	_____	_____
_____	_____	_____	_____

Equipment or Software Needed	Estimated Cost
_____	_____
_____	_____
_____	_____
_____	_____
_____	_____

FIELDS YOUR DATABASE NEEDS TO MANAGE

Your donor database guides your solicitation and leadership cultivation strategies. These are the categories of what is most often most relevant to know. (Never put highly sensitive information in your database.)

Primary
Name(s)
Primary home address
Secondary home address
Office address
Contact numbers: telephone and fax for office and
    home e-mail

Relationship to Your Organization
Gift history or last gift
Largest gift and purpose
Past solicitation results
Estimated capacity for giving
Estimated likely gift to your organization
Existing links to your organization
Board service with your organization; years of service
Officer positions held
Known sympathies for your cause
Best person(s) to cultivate or solicit them
Codes: A = ready to make a major gift
        B = needs some cultivation before a
            solicitation
        C = cold prospect (begin to cultivate)

Professional
Profession(s)
Company information (background, Web address)
Professional memberships and affiliations

Personal
Age, birthday, place of birth, where grew up
Schools and degrees earned

Awards and honors
Family information
Spouse or partner
Spouse or partner's profession
Previous marriages
Number and ages of children; their schools
Parents; other relatives of interest
Pets
Social and club memberships; affiliations
Hobbies and interests
Travel interests

Assets
Source(s) of wealth
Annual income
Stocks and bonds holdings
Principal home value
Other homes and real estate holdings value
Family foundation(s)
Other assets
Will made?
Other planned or deferred gifts arranged?
Estimated net worth

Community
Contributions to other organizations
Other board memberships and officer positions

Evaluations
Gift potential: outright? deferred?
Timing?
Cultivator or solicitor assigned; date of assignment

Establishing Effective Communications Channels

Clear and effective communications channels must be put in place. The goal of a good communications plan should be to inspire the members of all the groups with a stake in the organization and its success to get motivated and involved with your campaign and stay that way.

For the internal constituents of your organization to become galvanized by the campaign, they must indeed feel like insiders—the first to know. For the external people to become caught up in the campaign, they, too, must feel as though they are being treated like insiders. Everyone has to be in on the act somehow. To pull this off requires some advance planning.

You will need to identify all the people with whom you plan to communicate during the campaign and work out an overall plan for smooth and timely connections. What are the best methods for reaching each type of group? Meetings? E-mail? Telephone tree? And how often? Weekly? Monthly? As events unfold?

How the campaign leadership, both staff and volunteer, communicates with all groups as well as with each other is central to having a good experience. What quality of communication is important to achieve with each group? Warm and friendly? Brisk and businesslike? Narrative reports with pictures? Charts and bullet points?

The sample chart in Exhibit 2.1 shows one basic approach. Down the side are examples of various groups (constituencies) you will want to keep well informed and inspired during the campaign. Across the top are columns for the types of communication you might use. Information in the chart's cells can show timing, quality, or responsibility for each type of communication for a given group or person.

The chart in Exhibit 2.1 contains sample data to show how it can be used. Exhibit 2.2 is blank. You can use it to plan your communications.

Remember to budget for communications. Prepare a trial budget for your communications plan. Will additional staff be needed to support communications properly?

The following charts can help you estimate costs. The chart in Exhibit 2.3 contains sample data. Use the blank chart in Exhibit 2.4 for your own planning.

EXHIBIT 2.1
Sample Communications Planning Chart

BUILDING OUR DREAM: Campaign for the Future

COMMUNICATIONS PLANNING
(exclusive of solicitation packages)

SAMPLE CHART–MUST BE CUSTOMIZED

Chief communicators include:	Abbr:
Executive director	ED
Chief development officer	CDO
Campaign director/manager	CD
Campaign chair	CC
Campaign consultants	CSLT
Director media relations	DMR

(All communicators must stay in close communication!)

TYPES OF CONTACT	Minutes Hard copy/E-mail	Telephone Updates	In-Person Updates, Visits	Personal Letter Updates	Site Tours	Cultivation Events	Web Site	Press Kits	Campaign Bulletin (Quarterly)
CONSTITUENCIES:									
Campaign leadership									
(Co-)chairs	✓	Frequent/ED+	ED/CDO	ED/CC/CSLT	✓	✓	✓	✓	ALL
Campaign cabinet	✓	✓		CC/CD/CSLT	✓	✓	✓	✓	
Subcommittee members	✓			CC/CD/CSLT	✓	✓	✓		
Honorary council			ED/CDO	ED/CDO	✓	✓	✓		ALL
Board of directors									
Board chair/president	✓	Frequent	✓	✓	✓	✓	✓	✓	
Executive committee	✓	✓			✓	✓	✓		
Development committee chair	✓	Frequent		✓	✓	✓	✓	✓	
Development committee	✓				✓	✓	✓		
Full board	via board minutes				✓	✓	✓		ALL

Staff constituencies								
Program directors	✓	Frequent	✓	Group letter	✓	✓	✓	ALL
Staff members			✓					
Campaign Donors						✓	✓	ALL
Prospects								
Annual donors of $500+				Group letter	✓	✓	✓	YES
Program participants or beneficiaries, members, etc.				Group letter	poss.	✓		
Community Leaders and Groups								
Rotary Clubs			✓ ✓		✓	✓		
Elected officials					CD/ED/DM	✓		✓
Media			✓			✓	✓	
Features editors/writers		DMR			Dates		✓	
Features freelances								
Publishers				ED	C/ED/DMR			✓
All contacts					Kickoff/date			

EXHIBIT 2.2

Your Own Communications Planning Chart

COMMUNICATIONS PLANNING

(exclusive of solicitation packages)

Chief communicators include:	Abbr:
Executive Director	ED
Chief Development Officer	CDO
Campaign Director/Manager	CD
Campaign Chair	CC
Campaign Consultants	CSLT
Director Media Relations	DMR

TYPES OF CONTACT	Minutes Hard copy/ e-mail	Telephone Updates	In-person Updates, Visits	Personal Letter Updates	Site Tours	Cultivation Events	Web Site	Press Kits	Campaign Bulletin (quarterly)		
CONSTITUENCIES:											
Campaign Leadership											
(Co-)Chairs											
Campaign cabinet											
Subcommittee members											
Honorary Council											
Board of Directors											
Board Chair/President											
Executive Committee											
Development Committee Chair											
Development Committee											
Full Board											

Staff constituencies																										
Program directors																										
Staff members																										
Campaign Donors																										
Prospects																										
Annual donors of $_____																										
Community Leaders and Groups																										
Media																										

EXHIBIT 2.3

Sample Chart for Estimating Costs

	A	B	C	D	E	F	G	H	I	J	K
1	ESTIMATING COSTS OF A COMMUNICATIONS PROGRAM										
2											
3											Estimated
4	COST FACTORS:	No. of	Frequency	Materials	Rate* or Postage	Preparation Costs	Cost per Year	Staff Hours Required for	Rate	Cost of Time	Cost
5		Units	(times/year)	(per pc.)	(per pc.)	(per pc.)**	$(B \times C) \times (D+E+F)$	Each Event	($/hr.)	$(C \times H \times I)$	$(G+J)$
6	TYPE OF COMMUNICATION:										
7											
8	Survey development		1					15	30	$ 450	$ 450
9											
10	Personalized mailings	500	3	$0.10	$ 0.33	$ 0.25	$ 1,020	20	30	1,800	2,820
11											
12	Postcard	1,000	4	0.05	0.20	0.15	1,600	10	30	1,200	2,800
13											
14	E-mail***	Any number	15	–	–	–	0	4	30	1,800	1,800
15											
16	Telephone	500	3	0.00	0.10	0.00	150	10	30	900	1,050
17											
18	Newsletter	5,000	4	0.15	0.15	1.50	36,000	25	30	3,000	39,000
19											
20	Advertising	1	12	0.00	6,000	250.00	75,000	6	30	2,160	77,160
21											
22	Web site design							Contract			30,000
23											
24	Web site maintenance		12					10	30	3,600	3,600
25											
26											
27											
28											

*Rate multiple per column inch or other measure. Example given = 20 column inches at $300/inch.

**Preparation costs include mail house costs, labels, photography and camera-ready copy preparation, printing, etc.

***Does not count initial set-up time to enter e-mail addresses.

EXHIBIT 2.4

Your Chart for Estimating Costs

	A	B	C	D	E	F	G	H	I	J	K
								F–R			
1	ESTIMATING COSTS OF A COMMUNICATIONS PROGRAM										Estimated
2											
3					Rate* or	Preparation	Cost per	Staff Hours	Rate	Cost of	Cost
4	COST FACTORS:	No. of	Frequency	Materials	Postage	Costs	Piece	Required for	Rate	Time	
5		Units	(times/year)	(per pc.)	(per pc.)	(per pc.)**	$(B \times C) \times (D+E+F)$	Each Event	($/hr.)	$(C \times H \times I)$	$(G+J)$
6	TYPE OF COMMUNICATION:										
7											
8	Survey development										
9											
10	Personalized mailings										
11											
12	Postcard										
13											
14	E-mail										
15	Initial e-mail data entry										
16											
17	Telephone										
18											
19	Newsletter										
20											
21	Advertising										
22											
23	Host costs										
24											
25	Other costs										
26											
27	Web site design										
28											
29	Web site maintenance										

*Rate multiple per column inch or other measure. Example given = 20 column inches at $300/inch.

**Preparation costs include mail house costs, labels, photography and camera-ready copy preparation, printing, etc.

Establishing Visibility

Have you established visibility within your target donor communities? Remember that a new friend (cold prospect), no matter how enthusiastic about your presentation, will likely give at most half what an old friend will give. If you have to explain who you are and what you do and why it matters, you are not going to get as much.

➤ How Visible Are You?

Do you think your campaign prospects know what you really do, how you do it, and how effective you are?

Yes_____   No_____   Somewhat_____

Place your organization on the following list for each of the constituencies you identified on your communications planning chart (Exhibit 2.2). Copy the list as many times as necessary. In addition, if your donors tend to fall into clearly identifiable groups (by profession, by geography, by interest), judge how you show up with each.

Name of Constituency or Donor Group: _____

_____Your prospects get regular exposure to the nature of, need for, and quality of your work by people they have come to trust and admire.

_____Your prospects can talk about the importance of your type of work but don't really know anyone who works there or who is involved with it.

_____Your prospects can say what you do but can't say why your work is truly important.

_____Your prospects have heard of you but are not certain what you really do.

_____You do not even register on your prospects' radar.

What can you do to increase your visibility? First and foremost, you want to bring your best prospects in on the ground floor. Lead gift prospect cultivation and development occurs during the preparatory phase.

Engage your best prospects, including board members and prospective board members, in critical path planning sessions. Remember that prospects for major gifts who have critical responsibilities are your first resource for gifts to seed or lead off a campaign. Leaders with resources who make sizable lead-off gifts set the scale and the pace of the campaign. Similarly, when leaders with resources are unwilling to commit stretch gifts, they signal others to hold off also.

Screen for prospective leadership when preparing for a campaign. Look for leadership in this order:

Engage Leadership

Ways to engage leadership and lead prospects during the strategic planning phase could include steering committee meetings, long-range planning committee meetings, full board retreats, town meetings, and synthesis team meetings (this group must reconcile program vision with budgetary considerations).

During project planning, engage leaders and prospects in the site or building committee, marketing committee, program committee, project advisory board (invite the members to weigh in on plans at key points, either individually or as a group), selection of architectural firm(s), or selection of contracting firm(s).

Invite prospects to participate in a feasibility study or "campaign planning study." At a minimum, the twenty-five to thirty top prospects for lead gifts to the campaign should be visited as part of an independently conducted, professional planning study.

Ask prospects to participate in neighborhood meetings.

Meet the Neighbors

Many building projects bring change to their neighborhoods. Invite selected prospects to public sessions for your neighbors or prospective neighbors. These meetings inform the neighborhood about your project and address their concerns about traffic and parking, noise, possible pollution controls, and so forth. Without such sessions, you may face unexpected local opposition to your project.

Step Up Public Relations

Review and strengthen your marketing and public relations programs. A professional PR department can place stories about your organization where prospects will see them. Seeing is often believing. Stories are really all we have to get our messages across. Your PR people are vital to the telling.

Along with your newsletter and bulletin mailings, set up (or refine) and use your Web site effectively. Increasingly, donors will expect to find the answers to their questions on your site, and you had better be ready for them. (For further information, see Kristof and Satran, 1995, and Lee, 2000.)

Paying for Building Your Organization's Capacity

The elements needed to bring an organization to a new level of effectiveness or reach can be costly. Sometimes the challenge lies in financing the staff and consultant time needed to focus on planning. Sometimes the need includes training and education: board development for volunteers, fund raising, general management, and personnel management for staff. Sometimes you may need to hire more qualified staff but need some seed funding.

Many foundations are sensitive to the pressures on organizations to develop as professional institutions capable of planning and managing their futures and will accept proposals for "capacity building." These types of funds, however, are unusual and are most often forthcoming from funders with whom you have already developed a solid relationship.

ROSSO'S CAPITAL CAMPAIGN TEST FOR READINESS

The organization ready to embark on a campaign will have

- A history of strong volunteer leadership

- An involved, contributing, informed board of directors

- A strong history of gift support

- A history of doing a good job

- Established visibility within the target donor communities

- Prospects for campaign leadership

- Potential big gift contributors

- An identifiable constituency, including likely supporters for the cause

- A plan to develop a good prospect list

- A sound plan for the future

- A convincing statement of case, needs, and goals drawn from the plan

- Ability to support the campaign by knowledgeable staff

- A sound communications plan for all constituents

Testing for Project Readiness

Developing a Rationale for the Project

Getting Buy-In and Commitment from Internal Constituencies

Getting Ready for a Bricks-and-Mortar Project

What Costs Will We Encounter and When?

Obtaining Up-Front Planning Costs

Answering Important Questions

Understanding the Role of In-Kind Donations

Launching the Project

YOUR ORGANIZATION has leadership, a good record, and a sound methodology for planning. And your community is behind you. But will your community want to fund your plans for their money?

You may be asking people for the largest single gift they have ever made to your institution. Donors who didn't ask hard questions before may suddenly become your toughest critics. If you are not ready for their queries about how you would actually be spending the campaign proceeds, they are likely to withhold the gift you need.

For the sake of simplicity, the term *project* in this chapter refers to the ultimate destination for the campaign funds raised. The object of your campaign—the project—could be one or more buildings, various renovations, an endowment fund, quasi-endowment funds, equipment, or all of these together. Now let's get your project campaign-ready.

Testing for Project Readiness

Is everyone agreed on the purpose of your campaign? Are all of your constituents (board, program staff, administrative and development staff, loyal donors) agreed that the project is necessary? Does everyone agree that the same set of clear purposes will be served? Does everyone agree on who will be the beneficiaries of the project or what will be the outcomes?

Test for Agreement on Purpose
Take an inventory of your constituents or stakeholders, that is, people or agencies who have a stake in your organization by virtue of their investments or receipts of time, money, services, or career.

▬▬▬▶ Project Readiness Inventory

Score your estimate of your constituents' agreement to the *purposes* of the capital project like this:
Opposed = 0; Poorly Informed = 1; Lukewarm = 2; Agree, Ready, and Trusting = 3; Ardently in Agreement = 4.

If you believe—or know—that one or more of your lead gift prospects opposes or remains poorly informed, count that score twice (although three times might be nearer the mark).

List Your Constituents	Score (0–4)	
Board of directors	_____	
Staff administrative leadership	_____	
Program-project-academic leadership	_____	
Lead gift prospects	_____	
Total:	_____	Your Average Score: _____

If you got an average score lower than 3, you are not ready to launch your campaign.

Test for Agreement on Project Profile

Does your leadership agree to the project profile? Does leadership agree on the *scale and character* of your envisioned project?

▬▬▬▶ Scoring Enthusiasm for the Project

Use the same 0-to-4 scale to score their agreement and commitment. Again, if you believe—or know—that one or more of your lead gift prospects opposes or remains poorly informed about the scale of your project, count that score twice.

List Your Leadership Groups	Score (0–4)	
Board of directors	_____	
Staff administrative leadership	_____	
Program-project-academic leadership	_____	
Lead gift prospects	_____	
Total:	_____	Your Average Score: _____

If you got an average score lower than 3, you are not ready. You need to go back to the drawing boards to get enthusiastic agreement from your leadership on the scope of the project you envision.

Test for Agreement on Location

Have you determined the location or probable location for the project? *Location* can refer to a physical site for bricks and mortar, a Web site for an Internet project, an investment house or broker for endowment, and so forth. Does your leadership and your primary prospect group like *where* your envisioned project can be?

▶ Scoring Enthusiasm for Location

Use the same 0-to-4 scale for scoring their agreement and enthusiasm:

List Your Constituents	Score (0–4)	
Board of directors	_____	
Staff administrative leadership	_____	
Program-project-academic leadership	_____	
Lead gift prospects	_____	
Essential constituent membership (for example, a school's parent body or a library's user group)	_____	
Total:	_____	Your Average Score: _____

If you got an average score lower than 3, you are a long way from being ready. If educating your leadership on the merits of the location does not work, you may simply need to find an alternate location.

Developing a Rationale for the Project

The rationale for your project should encompass every hard question you can imagine that a serious prospective donor might ask. Your answers to these questions will help you build that rationale and prepare for the tough meetings.

▶ Answering the (Inevitable) Hard Questions

Answer each of the following questions in one hundred words or less. Organize detailed backup for each description.

What need does your organization address?

What's your organization's particular focus on addressing this need? How does your project help this focus?

How is your organization positioned to do this capital work?

How are your staff and board leadership qualified to do the work?

What are your goals for growth? Why is growth important?

How does your project enable your growth goals? Why is it needed?

Why does *this* project meet the need and not a different project?

How is this approach cost-effective?

How is your organization qualified to manage the project?

Why does this project need to occur now? Can't it wait a bit?

What will it cost? How are the cost estimates being developed? (How can I trust that they will hold within range?)

How does the organization plan to sustain its operations once the project is complete?

Getting Buy-In and Commitment from Internal Constituencies

A healthy campaign needs the support of the entire team. It is critical that the people who actually carry your organization day to day—those who bring your services to those you serve—think that the project (and its associated campaign) is a sound idea. Like the institutional plan on page 47, here is a workplan to ensure that your internal constituents have bought into the *project* plan.

Building the Internal Team

Who are your internal constituent groups?

_____

_____

_____

_____

_____

Which of these would be key to directing or helping to realize the envisioned project?

_____

_____

_____

_____

_____

Which of these would be key to encountering and talking with key donors during the campaign?

_____

_____

_____

_____

_____

Which of these would be key to keeping annual contributed income in balance during a campaign?

_____

_____

_____

_____

_____

From these quizzes you should be able to see the importance of having your entire team on board with your project. Let's review for a moment the planning steps concerning your team and project readiness.

Assessing Your Team's Buy-In

Can you really say that your internal team is on board?

Did you include all key internal constituencies in your strategic planning process for setting goals and objectives?

Yes_____   No_____   Somewhat_____

Have they agreed to and adopted the goals and objectives of the strategic plan?

Yes_____   No_____   Somewhat_____

Do internal constituencies now agree that the organization needs the project that would be the subject of a campaign?   Yes_____   No_____   Somewhat_____

Knowing the needs, do they agree that a capital campaign is a good idea? (One does not always follow from the other!)   Yes_____   No_____   Somewhat_____

If you answered "No" or "Somewhat" to any of these questions, you will need to step back in your process and consult with your constituents.

At this point you might see the need to build consensus. If so, arrange meetings for appropriate groups, at convenient times, with appropriate preparation.

Establishing Forums for Agreement

Talk with the key people. With what you have learned from their input, convene appropriate groups in the settings most conducive to two-way communication.

Are there acknowledged leaders within various staff groups?   Yes_____   No_____   Not sure_____

Who are they?

_____

_____

_____

Which individuals would it be wise to consult with one-on-one?

_____

_____

Convene your internal leadership to design the best kinds of gatherings. What forums are best for meetings, educational sessions, and participation?

_____

_____

_____

_____

Getting Ready for a Bricks-and-Mortar Project

To carry through a bricks-and-mortar project with success, you will need know-how in many areas. For example, you will need to know how to

- Develop a comprehensive budget.
- Weigh the benefits and drawbacks of renting as opposed to buying.
- Analyze your financial status, options, and potential.
- Select and retain the right people for your facility project team, including the architect, the project manager, and the builder.
- Negotiate a contract for construction.
- Maintain control of your project costs.
- Work with a space planner and architect.
- Work with contractors.

For these areas, you will need to turn elsewhere to gain expertise. This book will not tell you how to work with an architect or how to become a good financial planner. But do understand that if you lose control of your project costs, you may also lose your campaign. Therefore, the first items in the sequencing list call for gaining some wisdom and skills before you plunge in. The other items may loop back on themselves, or you may take them in somewhat different order out of necessity. Generally, however, here is how it goes:

- Sharpen your financial planning skill set.
- Locate some workshops, mentors, or volunteers who can coach you through the early phases of design, permits, cost estimates, and contract negotiations.
- Complete your use plan, that is, analyze your space needs for each program objective. If your building or land area is complex, the use plan may be called a master plan.
- Locate a suitable site or sites.
- Analyze all feasible site or renovations options.
- Engage an architect for preliminary design work.
- Work with the architect, as appropriate, to match space needs with a design layout that offers numerous opportunities for donors to name sections or rooms of the structure.
- Ensure that program and support personnel will not outgrow the planned space too quickly.
- Estimate cost ranges.

- Investigate financing resources, including bond issues.

- Secure the site; get permissions, permits, environmental impact reports (EIRs), neighborhood acceptances.

- Research code and permit requirements.

- Determine the cost impact of special code work.

- Engage architects for detailed design work.

- Engage an engineering architect to complete engineering drawings.

- Conduct the search for a contractor.

- Negotiate detailed construction budget and limits with the contractor.

- Determine what money might be saved with donated materials and time, and with discounts.

- Sign the contract with the contractor.

- Ask your architects to create renderings, sketches, or architectural models, as appropriate.

- Arrange for loans (short-term loans will pay for the project while the campaign pledges are being collected; long-term loans are fifteen- to thirty-year notes that your institution can pay off with increased annual income over many years).

- Retain a construction manager.

The last step is to retain a contract manager. On-staff executives often play this role. A contract manager monitors all money-related decision making, including "change orders" during the construction. (Change orders are requests to the contractor to build something differently from or in addition to what the signed contract specifies.) The contract manager also manages the time line, as well as all other aspects of the legal contract.

What Costs Will We Encounter and When?

It is useful to list all of the types of expenses that you may encounter, organized by phase of the project. Exhibit 3.1 breaks out which expenses you are likely to need to plan and prepare for and when they arise. As best you can, start putting expense numbers after each item that will apply to you.

EXHIBIT 3.1

Cost Categories for the Bricks-and-Mortar Capital Campaign

	A	B	C	D
		Year 1	Year 2	Year 3
2	**BEFORE THE CAMPAIGN**			
3				
4	**Plans**			
5	Institutional strategic plan			
6	Design and development of new programs and initiatives			
7	Institutional operating postconstruction budget			
8	Facilities plan			
9	Planning workshops			
10	Board retreats: hosting, facilitator, travel, and so on			
11	Communications plan			
12	Financial plan for entire project and campaign			
13	Allocated staff time			
14	Other			
15	**SUBTOTAL: PLANS**			
16				
17	**Capital Project Preparation**			
18	Architectural designs			
19	Realtor, site search			
20	Legal fees			
21	Environmental impact reports			
22	Neighborhood education, polling, meetings			
23	Traffic and parking assessments			
24	Engineering drawings, schematics			
25	Architectural models			
26	Allocated staff time			
27	Other			
28	**SUBTOTAL: PROJECT PREPARATION**			
29				
30	**Campaign Preparation**			
31	Seed fund development, consultant fees			
32	Donor and prospect cultivation and communications			
33	Feasibility study			
34	Advance or down payment fund			
35	Allocated staff time			
36	Other			
37	**SUBTOTAL: CAMPAIGN PREPARATION**			
38				
39	**TOTAL PRECAMPAIGN COSTS**			

EXHIBIT 3.1

Cost Categories for the Bricks-and-Mortar Capital Campaign, Cont'd.

	A	B	C	D
		Year 1	Year 2	Year 3
40	**DURING CONSTRUCTION AND CAMPAIGN**			
41				
42	**Acquisition Costs·**			
43	Land			
44	Structures			
45	Occupancy or air rights			
46	Other			
47	(*less advance fund, line 34)			
48	**SUBTOTAL: ACQUISITION**			
49				
50	**Construction Costs**			
51	Capital project management plan			
52	Contractor estimate or bid			
53	Additional materials			
54	Contract or construction manager			
55	Insurance			
56	Other			
57	**SUBTOTAL: CONSTRUCTION**			
58				
59	**Carrying Costs**			
60	Construction loan and loan fees			
61	Loan carrying costs			
62	Interest income lost			
63	Other interest payments on loans			
64	Other			
65	**SUBTOTAL: CARRYING COSTS**			
66				
67	**Operating and Logistical Costs**			
68	Rental costs during displacement			
69	Lost revenues during closure or displacement			
70	Long-term storage			
71	Other			
72	**SUBTOTAL: OPERATING COSTS**			
73				
74	**Endowment Funds**			
75	**Reserve Funds**			
76				

EXHIBIT 3.1

Cost Categories for the Bricks-and-Mortar Capital Campaign, Cont'd.

	A	B	C	D
		Year 1	Year 2	Year 3
77	**Fund Raising Costs**			
78	New equipment			
79	Additional staff positions			
80	Consultant fees			
81	Case and marketing materials			
82	Cultivation, host expenses, events			
83	Communications			
84	Travel			
85	Pledge attrition			
86	Allocated staff time			
87	Other			
88	**SUBTOTAL: FUND RAISING COSTS**			
89				
90	**Other Institutional Costs**			
91	Administrative staff time allocated to the project			
92	Other new staff positions			
93	Overhead additions			
94	**SUBTOTAL: INSTITUTIONAL COSTS**			
95				
96	**TOTAL PROJECT AND CAMPAIGN COSTS**			

Obtaining Up-Front Planning Costs

Clearly, to accomplish everything on your list requires a lot of time and expense—more than many organizations think may be needed. But the planning is essential. Without it, prospective donors have nothing to see, nothing to go on. Clearly, the expense involved in bringing a project to the starting line can be great. Where can this money come from? It can come from several sources. You will need to try the combination that is right for your organization. Here are three possible sources:

• *Board of directors' start-up fund.* Board members make gifts above and beyond annual giving just for this purpose. Any gift made to a start-up fund should be counted with a later capital gift for recognition purposes. Such funds go by many different names. "Seed fund," "nucleus fund," and "leadership fund" are some examples.

- *Grants.* Some foundations will make planning grants to organizations they know well and have learned to trust.
- *Loans.* Outside loans for planning are somewhat risky; at the time the loan is needed, there may be uncertainty that the project and a campaign will proceed at all. Some large institutions may make intra-organizational loans to advance its projects; universities are one example.

Answering Important Questions

People (your hoped-for donors) will ask all sorts of pesky questions about your project, but they're only pesky, really, if you haven't thought of them already and prepared answers. When you have the answers already in hand, it's wonderful to get questions because each one gives you an opportunity to confirm with your giving prospect that you have your act together.

Here are some of the most common questions people ask about brick-and-mortar projects. Test yourself. See if you can answer them.

Common Questions About Bricks-and-Mortar Projects

Fill in your best answers:

Why do we have to buy or build? Wouldn't it be better to rent? (Can't you build an addition instead of moving?)

Why does the project have to be this ambitious?

Why do you need this much space?

Why do we have to move on this project now? Why can't it wait?

Why does the project have to be in this location? Aren't there cheaper alternatives?

Why does the project have to have this configuration?

Why does the project have to cost this much?

How do you know your cost estimates will hold?

What are your provisions for ongoing maintenance of the property? How will the operations fund be protected from both maintenance and debt service requirements?

What are you doing about access?

What are you doing about parking?

What are you doing about security?

How long will it take to build? When would we have occupancy?

Here are questions people ask about a permanent fund campaign.

Common Questions About Endowment Projects

Again, test yourself. See how easily you can answer these questions:

Why raise ten times the amount we need for current purposes in order to build an endowment fund? We need vigorous, ongoing funding for operations, which is hard enough to do.

Why do we need to raise so much? What real difference will these funds make?

How will these funds be managed? Does the board of directors have a set of investment policies?

Whose professional investment practices and experience are you asking me to trust?

Can I be sure that these funds will be ethically managed?

How can I be sure that my "permanent" gift will indeed be honored and used for the purposes for which I gave it?

Do you have to have a full-fledged campaign to raise this money? What about a focus simply built in to ongoing fund raising, or grants, or a bequest program?

Understanding the Role of In-Kind Donations

Often, significant savings can be gained on a construction or project budget by soliciting outright or buying on discount major materials or time. The relationships you cultivate with potential suppliers can be worth huge savings. Treat them as you would a potential donor, and offer them donor-level recognition for the profits and principal they forgo.

Take another look at the pro forma budget you have just constructed. Now mark each line item for which you think significant ($10,000 or greater) in-kind savings might be attained.

Write here where you think such savings might come from.

Savings from In-Kind Donations and Discounts

Category	Prospects	Potential Savings

What Is a Feasibility Study?

Do You Need a Study?

What You Can Learn from a Study

How to Get Ready for a Feasibility Study

How to Time the Study

How to Find the Right Consultant

Cost of a Feasibility Study

Risks of Not Undertaking a Study

Alternatives to a Feasibility Study

Conducting a Feasibility Study

YOU BELIEVE your organization is strong enough to undertake a campaign. You've prepared your project. Now, are your donors ready and willing to help you with extraordinary gifts above and beyond their annual giving? Are you confident that your loyal supporters, as well as new friends you may need, will rise to the occasion?

What if you are a start-up? You've collected lists of names, combed the address books of your board members, and compiled a list of likely foundations. But will they be caught up by your idea? Will they make the gifts you'll need?

Your "market" consists of just two simple elements: people (enough of them) and potential contributions (enough of them). When you have enough prospects who are ready to give you enough money, you can feel reasonably safe about going ahead with your campaign.

If you are confident that your preparation is sound and your prospects are ready, you may be in a position to forgo the cost and trouble of a formal market test. If you are not so sure, it is time to test your philanthropic market.

How do you find out whether people are ready to give? You commission a *confidential* market test—most commonly called a feasibility study. This test of your donors' likelihood of giving to your project also goes by other names such as Market Survey or Planning Study. The study should reveal the real strengths and weaknesses in your donor base in relationship to your proposed plans and should make recommendations either for proceeding to prepare your campaign or taking alternative steps.

Note that the organization that does not undertake such a study in this day and age is the exception. Most nonprofits are not in a position to gauge campaign readiness without experienced, objective, outside help. It is worth noting that The Fund Raising School encourages feasibility studies, except in the rarest of instances.

What Is a Feasibility Study?

A feasibility study assesses in three main ways your organization's capacity to conduct a campaign. It assesses (1) your infrastructure (volunteer structure, staff capacity and experience, office systems) in terms of providing support to a campaign, (2) the relative strength and appeal of your case, and (3) your prospective donors' readiness to provide adequate funds against a proposed goal, along with any conditions or circumstances that are likely to raise their gift levels.

A consultant, acting as an impartial third party, conducts a confidential survey of your support base. The consultant presents your proposed plans to your prospects and discusses their reactions, comments, and level of interest in financial terms. He or she then relays that information to the organization, but without attribution. Not only do you learn what level of funding might be leveraged through a campaign but you acquire extremely valuable information about what your donor *market* (no individual names) really wants from you that is most meaningful to them.

Soliciting your loyal donors' advance views of your plans is properly seen as a mark of respect on your part. Conducting such "respectful conversations," as they have been called, with your constituents is also good public relations, outreach, and cultivation.

The report you receive should include the findings from the study, the consultant's conclusions and recommendations, and suggestions for steps your organization should take next. A well-done report is a lengthy document, so the consultants should also prepare an executive summary that you can use with your study participants and other key constituents.

Studies often go by different names, depending on the primary question:

Should we even consider launching a campaign? (feasibility study)

How should we prepare for a campaign? (campaign planning study)

Are our donors ready to make exceptional gifts? How ready? (market study)

What do we need to do to strengthen our organization as we begin to build toward a campaign? (development audit or organizational assessment) (Note that such audits are not used in capital campaigns.)

Do You Need a Study?

You need a study when it is important to project future outcomes in a timely way.

Assessing Your Need for a Study

Which of the factors listed here are relevant to your organization? If you check *any* of the choices in Category A, you should commission a study. That includes the last item on the list. If your marks all fall into Category B, you *may* not need a study. Consider your choice carefully in light of the next section.

Time Frame

Category A:

_____The project *must* be completed within a time frame of a few years.

Category B:

_____The project *could* be completed over many years in stages.

_____The first stage of this project *must* be completed with early, leadership funds, but the balance *could* be completed in many stages over time.

_____The project *could* be completed in a build-as-you-go manner as special funds and budget surpluses are collected.

Resources Needed

Category A:

_____The campaign must raise a minimum amount of money or the overall purpose of the project will fail—or the project cannot be financed and should not be undertaken at this time.

_____The campaign must raise a minimum amount of money or the leadership won't think they can get behind it.

_____Advance communication with your major donors about major new works matters.

Category B:

_____The campaign must raise an unspecified amount of money to begin work on the project; subsequent funding can add to the project.

Leadership

Category A:

_____Leadership for this project will perform best within a defined period of special activity.

Category B:

_____Leadership for this project is likely to endure without burnout for many years.

Funding Levels

Category A:

_____Funding levels can likely not be assessed by talking with the individuals who already know our organization. New sources will have to be identified and solicited within the course of the campaign. But it doesn't matter; we have no choice but to proceed.

Category B:

_____Funding levels can probably be assessed by talking with individuals who already know our organization.

What You Can Learn from a Study

Institutional leaders may feel entirely comfortable about the loyalty of the donors to the institution, yet they may know little about how their donors actually regard the proposed project and associated campaign. Donors may be wonderful about giving to the annual campaign yet reluctant to give to the capital campaign.

Here are the key questions that a good study should answer:

Is your proposed goal in range? Do you have the lead gifts ready that will drive your campaign? What does the Table of Gifts (sometimes called the gift pyramid) look like for your proposed campaign? Do you have enough good prospects to support results of

1 gift at 10%–20% of goal?

2 gifts at 5% of goal?

4 gifts at 2.5% of goal?

8 gifts at 1% of goal?

What is the condition of your leadership? Do you have campaign leaders who can and will inspire, motivate, and galvanize major gifts? If not, what do you need to do to attract and cultivate such leaders?

Does your organization enjoy a positive image with those whom you will need to ask for all key types of support (contributions, underwriting, community acceptance, and so on)?

How strong is the appeal of your case? Are your prospects passionate about the cause? Do your prospects perceive your organization and your plans as nice-to-have or necessary? Are your plans timely and compelling to them? Do your naming opportunities have appeal?

Does your constituency have wealth enough to share enough? Are they likely to give the extra gift to you or to another organization in your field?

Is your infrastructure ready for a campaign?

Is the economic climate right for your capital campaign?

The report you get back from your consultants should contain clear answers to all these questions and cite original evidence (although quotes should never be attributed to their source).

Here are the key planning points a good study should provide. If the response has been strong enough, the report should guide your next steps for preparing your campaign with

- A recommended leadership structure
- Recommended names to provide leadership
- A time line
- Budget information
- Other organizational changes that could strengthen your chances, such as board growth or compositional change, development staffing, or record-keeping software changes

If the response was weaker than hoped for, the report should guide your next steps with recommendations that show you

- How you can strengthen your case (a weak case will affect the size and timing of major gifts and cause an anemic campaign)
- How you can change your image in the community
- How you can strengthen your relationships with your donors
- How you can strengthen your leadership (inappropriate or weak leadership, either staff or volunteer, will cause an anemic or failed campaign)
- Other organizational changes, such as board growth or compositional change, development staffing, or record-keeping software changes

In some instances an organization may simply have to face up to one of many possible realities:

- There are not enough qualified prospects (people or agencies with ready potential gifts) to come close to the goals.
- Constituents just disagree with the project, its scope, or its timing and won't provide the levels of funding that will be needed.
- A lot more preliminary work is needed to prepare aspects of the organization, or of the donor base, or both.

How to Get Ready for a Feasibility Study

Knowing that you want to commission a study may not mean that you are ready to proceed with one. Before you pay your consultant that retainer, make sure your timing is right to get the information you want to pay for. And you can get a jump on your time line. Draw on the prospect lists that you created in Chapter Two, and take the following readiness test. When your consulting firm comes on board, they should guide you through this process again.

Do you have sufficient prospects for the consultant to interview?

◄━━━━━━━━►Adding Up Your Prospects for a Study

Number your *key* constituents—those you believe are desirable to be surveyed for your project. Number of:

_____Board

_____Staff

_____Long-time donors

_____New donors

_____Potential new donors

_____Political figures

_____People in government administration

_____Community leaders

_____Total interview prospects

Do you have at least one hundred good names? If not, *stop!* You are not ready to proceed with a survey or study. You will be wasting time, money, and momentum to continue along a campaign path.

It is the common experience of capital campaigns that fewer than one hundred people (including funding from granting agencies) account for approximately 80 percent of the campaign revenue. Do you have eighty to one hundred prospects with the capacity and *potential* interest to make gifts adding up to 80 percent of the campaign goal you want to test? Let's see.

◄━━━━━━━━►Evaluating Your Study Prospects

How many prospects do you have who *could* (not would) make a gift that is 20 percent of the desired campaign goal? List them here, or you might prefer to create this list in your database or in a spreadsheet program.

Names   Conceivable Gift

_____

_____

_____

_____

_____

_____

Total number of prospects: _____   Total conceivable gifts: $ _____

How many prospects do you have who *could* (not would) make a gift that is 10 to 15 percent of the desired goal? List them:

Names   Conceivable Gift

_____

_____

_____

_____

_____

_____

_____

Total number of prospects: Total conceivable gifts: $ _____

How many prospects do you have who *could* (not would) make a gift that is 5 percent of the desired goal? List them:

Names   Conceivable Gift

_____

_____

_____

_____

_____

_____

_____

_____

Total number of prospects: Total conceivable gifts: $ _____

How many prospects do you have who *could* (not would) make a gift that is 1 percent of the desired goal? List them:

Names   Conceivable Gift

_____

_____

_____

_____

_____

_____

_____

_____

_____

_____

_____

_____

_____

_____

_____

_____

_____

_____

_____

_____

_____

_____

_____

Total number of prospects: _____   Total conceivable gifts: $ _____

How many prospects do you have whom you believe could be cultivated to make a major gift but you have no idea how to place them in a list like the foregoing? List them here:

Names   Representative Previous Gift (if any)

_____

_____

_____

_____

_____

_____

_____

_____

_____

_____

_____

_____

_____

_____

_____

_____

_____

_____

_____

Total number of prospects: _____   Total representative gifts: $ _____

Five lists, total number of prospects: _____   Total Conceivable Gifts: $ _____

Total Conceivable Gifts = _____ Percentage of $ _____ (Desired Campaign Goal)

Total Conceivable Gifts = _____ Percentage of $ _____ (80 Percent of Desired Campaign Goal)

_____

If you have between sixty and one hundred prospect names *and* the total for conceivable gifts is at least double the contemplated campaign goal, you have sufficient prospects to proceed with a campaign planning and market study.

What if you don't have enough prospects? Get help learning about your key prospective donor constituencies. Organize a few visits by board and executive staff. You will learn a great deal from the process of trying to get the visits as well as from the visits themselves. Your lack of prospects may also be tied to the relative strength of your board.

Staff Time

Do you have adequate staff time available to work with the consultants and your prospects? A new fund raising manager was heard to exclaim, "I never realized that hiring a consultant would require so much work from me!"

Consultants usually (and should) ask quantities of questions that only the client can answer. Once an organization embarks on a project of this magnitude, those in charge of fund raising can expect to put up to 30 percent of their time into preparing the study for a few months.

Credibility of Your Case

Your case needs to be ready for your prospects at this most sensitive stage of *prospect cultivation*—for a study functions as such. Your prospects are your toughest critics, and you'll want to look crisp, with your basic homework done before inviting your donors to render early judgment on your project and their chances of giving to it. As Hank Goldstein has often observed, "One reason not to give is as good as another."

Can you provide your prospects with enough detailed information in your story that they can react to it in a meaningful way? When consultants talk with prospective campaign donors during the planning phase, they must be prepared with succinct answers to the questions you answered in Chapter Three. In addition, they will need answers to a few more questions. Again, please provide your answers in one hundred words or less. Do you have detailed backup for each description?

Develop More Bullet Points for Your Case

What is the physical work planned? What will it look like?

Where will it be?

Who will benefit?

What is the history of the organization's contribution to the community/field/individual lives?

Who is leading this project?

Organizational Weaknesses
Does your organization have any of these weaknesses?
Here are examples of factors that can greatly weaken the return on investment for a study.

➤ Test for Efficient Use of Feasibility Study Costs

Check off which, if any, of these factors apply to your organization. If any do, wait as long as possible to strengthen your position before sending a consultant to talk with prospects.

_____ Rationale for the project is weak.

_____ Rationale for the goal is weak.

_____ No executive director is in place.

_____ The executive director is too new or unknown to prospects for them to know whether to place their confidence in either the director or in the director's ideas.

_____ Board leadership is in transition.

_____ Board of directors is too weak to lead the project.

_____ Board of directors is untutored about the capital campaign process and is either too eager or too cautious about proceeding.

_____ Board of directors is unknown to prospects.

_____Location of the project has yet to be determined.

_____Scope and cost dimensions of the project have yet to be determined.

_____Organization is newly recovering from a scandal.

_____Donors responding to previous solicitations have not been well "stewarded," that is, thanked and appreciated in a manner that is meaningful to them.

If any of these factors strike home, you do not want to pay a consultant to bring back information you already have about potential donors' negative or hesitant views. Well before bringing in a consultant, organize information-giving and advice-seeking thank-you visits by board and executive staff to your key prospective donors. You will gain (or regain) the respect of your best constituents, and you will learn a great deal about the preparatory steps you may still need to take.

Board Leadership

Ask yourself these two questions: (1) Is one of your greatest worries that your board of directors is simply unable or unwilling to lead a campaign? (2) Do you have little leeway for changing the composition or mind-set of the board?

If you answered either of these yes, then "just let them slumber," as Hank Rosso used to say. Look for ways to cultivate and create an alternative leadership group that can and will lead a campaign. Explore such a question in every one of your cultivation meetings with your constituents. Probe for possible group members.

During the campaign and after it has concluded, this alternative group can provide the board talent that can help you sustain the strength you have built.

How to Time the Study

People's personal circumstances and attitudes can change quickly. The best time to consult with them is after you have conceptualized and rationalized your planning, but before you have made your final decisions, and within six months of the time you want to proceed to the start-up phase of your campaign. Visiting a prospect sets up expectations that a gift request will proceed within a reasonably short time thereafter. A long lapse in communication can, ultimately, be counterproductive.

How to Find the Right Consultant

The right consultant for your organization will hold your confidence because he or she

- Knows the work and get results
- Has sympathy for your mission
- Will work well with your leadership
- Will work well with your staff

The steps that are outlined next for finding a qualified consultant have been tested over the years by members of the AAFRC (American Association of Fund-Raising Counsel). You should have a good result.

• *Step 1: Identify prospective consultants.* Begin by asking for referrals from board members or colleagues. Also check directories. The National Society of Fund Raising Executives (NSFRE) prints an annual directory of consultants, available from its Web site (http://www.nsfre.org) or by phone at (800) 666-3863. Some local chapters of the NSFRE also maintain consultant directories. The American Association of Fund-Raising Counsel (AAFRC) lists experienced campaign counsel in its national directory and on its Web site (http://www.aafrc.org), or you can call (317) 816-1613.

Another way to get information is to respond to listings in trade periodicals or the Yellow Pages of your telephone book.

• *Step 2: Conduct a preliminary screening.* One way to get basic information is to request it from each firm. Get an overview of their services. Then after you have narrowed the field to a maximum of three or four candidates, you need more detailed information. But interviewing more than four firms can become repetitive, frustrating, and too time consuming for staff and volunteers. Three firms are plenty.

Arrange a face-to-face briefing with each. It is not to your advantage to require a full proposal without the benefit of a briefing. To prepare for the briefing, you should furnish the following:

- Description of your organization
- List of your board of directors
- Your last annual report
- Your current board-approved budget
- The latest information about campaign funding needs or desires

• *Step 3: Request proposals.* After the briefing, request proposals from the firms you know you would like to continue with. Proposals should clearly state the costs, fees, services, and a preliminary schedule.

- *Step 4: Check references.* Always ask for references; always check them carefully. Ask clients whether they would hire the firm again.

  Ask for three references from satisfied clients and one reference from a client whose initial objectives were not achieved or when either the firm or the organization resigned from the contract. Firms should treat the fourth request as standard operating procedure.

- *Step 5: Understand chemistry.* There are many ways of knowing about a subject and of applying that knowledge when making a decision. You should try to be as objective as possible, using professional judgment and assessing your impressions carefully. Remember though that personal preferences are part of every professional relationship and every hiring decision. If you really do not relate well to someone when he or she is trying to impress you, chances are the relationship will not grow fonder.

- *Step 6: Notify candidates.* Notify all candidates of your decision. It is considered a courtesy to explain briefly the reasons for your choice to the consultants you did not select.

- *Step 7: Draw up a contract.* The contract is very important and should be specific and detailed. This is the best time to uncover and iron out specific expectations or misunderstandings. You may wish to consult legal counsel regarding specific, appropriate terms and their wording in the document. The following matters, as well as others recommended by the organization's board or legal adviser, should be elucidated in detail in a contract or a letter serving as a contract:

  - *Services:* What services will be provided? When and how often will you receive reports? What will they contain?

  - *Schedule:* If the time period is expressed in days, how many hours is the day? For a planning or feasibility study, when will it start, and when will it conclude?

  - *Fees:* What professional fees will be billed? What is the billing schedule? What additional expenses will be reimbursed by the client, up to what amount?

  - *Personnel:* Which people from the firm will provide direct services, and what other professionals may be called upon to support them?

  - *Fiscal responsibility:* Who in the organization is responsible for contractual decisions, and who is responsible for rendering payment?

  - *Location:* Will the services be rendered on-site or off-site?

Note that fees should always be based on services rendered. When you negotiate a contract for campaign management, never allow fees to be based on the goal of the campaign. Contingency fund raising is prohibited by premier firms and eschewed by ethical consultants.

Areas of Potential Difficulty

Changing Consultants

When you are ready to commence your campaign, the firm that conducted your study is usually the logical choice to engage for your campaign. But what if you want to change? Although changing consultants is a completely legal option and one appropriately exercised if you are truly dissatisfied, the firm that does your feasibility study or begins your campaign develops a knowledge of your organization and constituency that goes beyond the parameters of even the most thorough and detailed report. A great deal of accumulated wisdom is lost when bringing in a new firm midway through a process.

Evaluating the Lowest Bid

Each campaign should be designed specifically for your organization and should not be shaped with a cookie-cutter approach. Even responsible bids vary, and you have to use professional judgment and fact checking to know what you really want. Sometimes the lowest bid is the best one, but not necessarily.

Communicating with Donors

The relationship between a charity and its donors is precious and should continue long after counsel has left. Anything that comes between an organization and its constituency is detrimental to long-term viability and the organization's potential to fulfill its mission. Staff, board members, or volunteers—not counsel—should ask for donations. Written communications as well as verbal ones should be developed with scrupulous oversight from the organization.

Cost of a Feasibility Study

A feasibility or planning study can cost anywhere from $15,000 to several tens of thousands, depending on the geographical scope of the study, the number of people to be interviewed, the type or configuration of the organization, and a number of other factors.

A typical cost range for studies with straightforward preparation needs, limited scope, and thirty to fifty respondents is between $25,000 and $45,000.

It may be possible to obtain a grant to fund a feasibility study. Many foundations are sensitive to the need for certain kinds of organizations to raise this money up-front in order to get started, so they will respond positively. You should be prepared in case there is a shortfall between the cost of the study and the grant awarded.

You can count on those same foundations, however, to inquire about what investment the board of directors has made. If the necessary leadership for a campaign is to come from the board, the board must stand behind its own fund raising efforts and help make the case for such a need to the funder.

▶ Preparing Your Rationale for Funding

In the space that follows, try explaining why your board of directors or your operating budget will not be financing the preliminary costs associated with campaign preparation.

1. The funding for campaign preparation will need to come from outside sources because

A funder is likely to have a follow-up question. Be ready.

2. The board's strategy for fund raising leadership once such a grant has been awarded is

Risks of Not Undertaking a Study

Plunge in without knowledge at your peril. Blind faith is a wonderful comfort if you are not holding ultimate responsibility for the success or failure of a project.

Two primary factors generally tempt some boards away from the hard work of board and institutional development and careful campaign preparation: (1) faith alone that the money will come from *somewhere*, or the odd, big gift will come sailing in over the transom, and (2) construction deadlines necessitated by such things as natural disasters or building code changes.

Yet there are indeed circumstances in which the expense and trouble of a feasibility study may not be necessary or may be the wrong instrument for the moment.

Alternatives to a Feasibility Study

There are other ways to obtain information short of a full-scale feasibility study. In certain cases, money and time may be better spent elsewhere. Here are some alternatives and the conditions under which they may be the better course of action.

Experimental Campaign

You could explore conducting an abbreviated campaign with an achievable goal if any of these conditions apply:

- Your board has little history of giving, and a small campaign could jump-start new practices and understandings.

- Your plans are in good condition, and you have access to good prospects with an interest in your purposes.

- Your plans are in good condition, and a big contribution could launch a major gifts program for your organization.

- You see the possibility of bringing important new donors into your organization with the vehicle of a minicampaign and all its recognition opportunities for donors.

- Assuming your plans are in good condition and you have access to real prospects, you can use the success of a small campaign to demonstrate your ability to achieve results and leverage new giving for the next campaign.

Deep Pockets Campaign

In a small campaign, it may be possible that a few deep pockets can be enough to kick off your fund raising. You can explore launching a small campaign if

- You have reliable reason to believe that your existing leadership will provide at least 50 percent of the goal

- You have a large enough, loyal donor base with enough philanthropic capacity that you feel the momentum of a campaign can truly inspire them to carry you to the goal (and perhaps beyond).

Warning: never, never estimate what others will give your organization based solely on the amount of wealth you can see in the economy around you!

"We Know We're Ready" Campaign

If your organization can meet *all* of the following conditions, you may well be in a position to forgo a feasibility study.

Checklist of "All Ready" Conditions

Check all that apply to you:

_____You have a large, loyal donor base with whom you have long been in good communication, and who (you have reason to believe) will respond to the call.

_____Your research has clearly identified and evaluated one hundred prospects who are likely to make a major gift to the campaign. Together, the likely gifts from this group add up to about 80 percent of the hoped-for campaign goal.

_____Your plans are in good order, brought there with the involvement of key board leadership.

_____You have a core of committed board members (at least eight is good) who are strong contributors and solicitors. This group can and will open doors, make lead gifts, and get others to do the same.

_____The board membership as a whole has committed to learn the basics of good campaign planning and solicitation techniques and will drive this campaign with all its heart, beginning with their own pace-setting gifts.

_____The capital project or programs proposed can be staged and built in phases.

_____The organization's executive staff and development staff have gained the respect and confidence of its board and campaign leadership.

_____The development program operates smoothly and creatively.

_____You have developed an attractive program for recognizing gifts to the campaign.

_____The case for support has been tested with key individuals and found to be compelling, realistic, and effective.

SAMPLE CONTENTS OF A FEASIBILITY STUDY REPORT

The report a consultant submits will be customized for each situation. In general, however, you may expect to see the following topics addressed.

- Introduction
- Findings and recommendations
- The case for support
- Mission
- Campaign leadership
- Favorable fund raising factors
- Unfavorable fund raising factors
- Assessment of campaign potential
- Setting the goal
- Potential major donors
- Organizing the campaign
- Campaign leadership
- Campaign communications
- Donor recognition, privileges, and policies

- Staffing
- Summary of conditions requisite for the launch of a campaign
- Other factors that would enhance fund raising
- Role of the annual fund in the campaign
- Time line
- Visibility
- Campaign costs
- Other outcomes
- Summary
- Persons interviewed
- Excerpts from interviews
- Questionnaire used
- Study prospectus

Responding to the Results of the Feasibility Study

Deciding Next Steps

Setting a Campaign Goal

Preparing the Case Statement

Posing Questions to Leadership

Using the Test to Prepare for Volunteer Training

Thanking and Acknowledging Participants

CHAPTER 5

Building the Campaign Framework

YOU NOW HAVE the answers you need to a great many questions. You are ready for the final run-up to the campaign. With the information collected, you are ready to decide the scope of your campaign, to create a case statement highlighting the points that will resonate the most with your donors, to prepare your leadership to make that case, and to practice early donor stewardship (TLC) with your team.

Responding to the Results of the Feasibility Study

A feasibility study report usually contains much detailed information about how the organization can further strengthen its case to its prospective donors. There are several steps you need to take immediately:

- *Step 1: Distribute study results to the board.* Prepare or have prepared an executive summary of the feasibility study. The summary should highlight the study's major findings and major recommendations. Distribute the summary to every member of the board. Distribute the full report to the executive committee, at least, and to every other board member who would like one or should have one.

- *Step 2: Convene the board and consultants.* Convene the full board of directors, and ask the consultant to present the results of the study and discuss the recommendations with the board.

- *Step 3: Make and communicate a preliminary determination.* Timely, continuing communication with your study participants and key prospects at this juncture is extremely important. The board needs to prepare a brief letter thanking them again and letting them know how, and along what time frame, the organization plans to act on the recommendations of the study. A copy of the executive summary, provided it outlines positive next steps, could be sent as well.

Deciding Next Steps

It is time for the board and staff leadership to review all the information, assess the risks, and decide what to do.

Using all your information sources, including the feasibility study report if you have one, take the following test to help you decide how to proceed.

➤ **Assessment Quiz**

Score the following statements from 1 to 5, using 1 for Strongly Disagree and 5 for Strongly Agree.

Part One: The Foundations

1. Your organization is well known and respected by your community, including those who are most likely to support you. _____

2. The campaign case tests strongly with the community and is clear about how the new asset (endowment, building, and so on) will deliver needed benefits that donors care deeply about. _____

3. All members—100 percent—of the board have agreed to make personal gifts from their own assets and to open doors to others as they can. _____

4. You know where to find the first 30 percent of your proposed goal and who will solicit the gifts. _____

5. The CDO reports directly to the chief executive of the organization and has a mutually respectful working relationship. _____

6. The CDO ranks with executive management. _____

7. At least one senior person on the development staff has capital campaign experience. _____

   Score for Part One: _____

   Scoring on the foundations is necessarily rigorous. If you scored less than 32 on Part One, you already have cause for concern about proceeding immediately to a campaign.

Part Two: Leadership and Support

1. You know thirty to forty leaders in the community who are important to your organization; you can approach them for a lead or major gift, an endorsement, and for opening doors (all three). _____

2. The annual giving program has a major gifts component and has been strong and consistent. _____

3. Volunteer leadership has emerged and declared themselves ready and eager to begin. _____

4. Board leadership and the CDO have a responsive and mutually respectful relationship. _____

5. Board leadership and the organization's administration have a responsive and mutually respectful relationship. _____

6. Planning for the capital project and associated campaign was a cooperative effort between administrative staff, development staff, program staff, and board. _____

7. Executive staff view the campaign for the project as a priority for the organization. They are willing and able to give their time. _____

8. Professional and program staff (and program volunteers) understand the project and its campaign and support the effort. _____

Score for Part Two: _____

Combined Scores: _____

Here's what your scores mean:

65 to 75 points (with a score of at least 32 on Part One). The organization is ready to proceed with a campaign with a good chance of success. Review the possibility of hiring the services of a capital campaign firm relative to the capacity and experience of your development staff.

50 to 64 points. The organization is coming into position for a campaign but needs further planning and development.

40 to 49 points. There is much work to do. A challenging campaign goal is likely out of reach at this time.

Under 40 points. Do not think about a campaign. Think about laying down the basics for your organization.

Setting a Campaign Goal

When is it time to set a goal? We can find out. Check off whether you have met the following conditions.

►Checklist for Goal-Setting Readiness

When all items are checked, it is time to set the goal.

_____Feasibility study results have been received (a proposed goal will have been tested).

_____The study recommends moving ahead with a campaign (and the necessary conditions for moving ahead that are specified in the report have been met); the board concurs. The preceding test can be a guide.

_____Capital costs have been reliably estimated and a healthy contingency applied.

_____Phasing options have been researched.

Now follow the next eight steps to set a goal.

• *Step 1:* Delegate a small task force composed of both board and staff members to study conditions and make a recommendation on a goal to the board.

• *Step 2:* The task force should review the study report in its entirety and consider progress on any of the additional preparatory steps recommended.

• *Step 3:* The feasibility study report will have tested a preliminary goal and made a recommendation on a goal the consultants believe can be achieved. Compare the recommendations from the report with any major new information that may have surfaced since the completion of the report (double-check with the consultants to ensure that this information was not counted).

• *Step 4:* Study the materials and labor lists for a building project. Does the organization have connections for pro bono work or significant discounts on goods that could be factored against the projected costs?

• *Step 5:* Study the organization's past history in handling major projects. Is there a track record? Is it positive? Negative? A negative record would indicate the need to keep the goal a safe distance above the project cost estimates.

• *Step 6:* Study the realities involved in staging or phasing a project. Can certain achievable milestones be tied to achievable campaign phases? Would phasing create needed milestones and opportunities to stop and celebrate? Would phasing offer you an opportunity to return to certain key donors for a second (or third) gift?

• *Step 7:* Develop a proposed goal or goals and the number of proposed phases for the campaign. If either goal or phasing differs much from the recommendations in the report, ask your consultants if, given how you arrived at the figures, you are taking too large a risk or too little. Bear in mind that in many campaigns there is a small but significant percentage (5 percent or more) of people who pledge a gift but do not pay. Plan for it. Also there are a number of stories about donated properties or assets that were later contested by family members and went to litigation. But you need not anticipate such misadventures in your goal setting.

• *Step 8:* The task force presents the proposed goal and phasing to the board. The board then votes.

There can be a period of goal elasticity before a campaign launches. If dramatic news or events occur, then change your plans accordingly. Even later in a campaign, goals can be raised. This happens often, as it becomes apparent that more money can be raised.

Preparing the Case Statement

Using the information from the feasibility study, you are now in a good position to begin filling out and sharpening the case statement you will need in a campaign.

A case statement sets forth the rationale for funding your organization or project. If you have completed a comprehensive strategic or long-range planning project, all the elements you will need should be found there.

The term *case* in a legal context means "a convincing argument." However, we all know that outside the courtroom, reason alone may not convince. So a good case statement pulls together more good evidence *and* more touching stories to back your request than a potential funder can resist.

When you conduct a feasibility study with your best prospects, you will need to have as strong a case for them as you can present at the time. Your prospects' reactions to it will influence your campaign start-up preparations. As you go into a capital campaign, you should create at least four different versions of your case for a variety of purposes. Here is what you should have under your belt.

Your Capital Campaign Encyclopedia

This comprehensive document is the source to which you can return for basic information about every aspect of your project and your organization's role in carrying it off. It should provide answers to everything you can imagine that people would want to know before making that big donation.

Information About Your Organization's Mission and Vision

(See your answers in Chapter Three.)

- What specific need does your organization address?

- What's your organization's particular focus on addressing this need? How does your project help your focus?

- Is your organization well positioned to do this capital work?

- What are your goals for growth? Why is growth important?

Information About Your Project

- How does your project enable your growth goals?

- Why does *this* project meet the need and not a different one?

- How is this approach cost-effective?

- How is your organization qualified to manage the project?

- Why does this work need to occur *now*?

Information About Your Leadership

- How are your professional staff qualified to do the work?
- How is your board leadership ready and qualified to lead?

Other Useful Information

- Statistics about program effects
- Stories about how your organization has touched or changed lives or had the desired impact
- Testimonials from program participants (collect pictures, too)
- Testimonials from satisfied donors, funders, and board members
- Sketches, schematics, drawings, pictures of architectural renderings
- Copies of planning reports about the project
- Other materials as they contribute to the big picture

Your Capital Campaign Marketing Brochure

The printed piece sent to donors is often called the case statement. You can begin collecting both text and image ideas for the brochure throughout your preparation work. Advance thinking will serve the compressed time line that campaigns often face as organizations begin the countdown to launch.

Anything you use with donors must move the case out of the encyclopedia and into the heart. No one will take the time (except possibly government funding agents and new board members) to read your encyclopedia. The case you present to prospects must *move* them.

Moving people's hearts deserves a word apart. It requires clear writing, attuned graphics, and the ability to showcase your stories honestly, plainly, and compellingly. When Hank Rosso, founder of The Fund Raising School, visited capital campaign classes to lecture about case statements, he did not bring along copies of the latest tomes on how to raise money. No. He brought Richard Lederer's *Anguished English* (1989). Then he would plead with the class to write well-crafted stories *from the heart*. Briefly! And he would cite the sainted E. B. White, quoting William Strunk Jr. in *The Elements of Style* (1959, p. ix): "Make every word tell." As if that were not enough, the case statement for a capital campaign must also set the stage for great works. "If it conveys positive undeniable truths and exciting plans with a glow of confidence, it can become a dynamic tool," says Thomas E. Broce in *Fund Raising* (1986, p. 159). It is not surprising that organizations often hire professionals for this work.

Your One–Paragraph Rationale

You will have need to condense your rationale into one clear paragraph. In just a few sentences, you must hold your readers spellbound while you reprise these major elements from the encyclopedia:

1. The specific need your organization addresses.
2. Your organization's particular focus on addressing this need.
3. How your project furthers this work.
4. How your organization is best positioned to do this work.
5. Why this work needs to occur *now.*

Can you write a compelling rationale for funding your capital project in a few sentences? Here is an example to give you the flavor. This piece was written for the 125th anniversary campaign for the Bar Association of San Francisco (for combined capital, program, and endowment funding) in 1997:

> *The 125th Anniversary and the creation of a new Bar Center in the historic Merchants Exchange Building provide a magnificent opportunity. There is no better way to honor our historic commitment to excellence, to equality of opportunity, and to access for all to our system of justice than to lay the cornerstone for the next generation of innovation and dedication. The Bar Association of San Francisco holds an important place in our professional lives. The Association is our professional home—the place which mentored us as young attorneys—the place where we seek out one another professionally and socially—the place where the poor and disenfranchised turn for help when hope fails them. The success of the 125th Anniversary Campaign will be a success shared by all.*
>
> *Donors will be honored at a private reception just before the Anniversary Gala. A distinguished group of notables and colleagues will be there. Your firm should be present to be recognized along with the other prominent members of our Bar Association.*

Now you try it—on your own paper this time!

Your "Elevator Speech"

You step into an elevator on the fifteenth floor, and there is a colleague you have had in mind for the campaign. You have just the ride down to the lobby to present your case. The under-one-minute speech is perhaps most important case treatment on your shelf. It is often the most challenging of all because of the need for brevity. And because it is used in person, it's the most powerful. All of your volunteers and staff need to be equipped with the one-minute speech for those brief encounters of the prospect kind.

Try this as an exercise. Record (transcribe) a compelling description of your capital project and rationale for funding it in a few conversational sentences.

Find a friend or colleague and a tape recorder. Read what you wrote for your One-Paragraph Rationale, put the copy down, turn on the tape recorder, and have your friend ask you, "So, what are you up to these days?"

Write down what you said. Repeat this procedure until you—and others—are satisfied.

Posing Questions to Leadership

You have completed your project and organizational readiness steps, and you have worked through how to present the rationale for your project. It is time to focus on getting your leadership ready to carry the case themselves and to develop the specialized fund raising role they will be taking on. What will they say to their colleagues and associates and friends to make them enthusiastic about your venture? As you know, your volunteers often won't have much time to get the attention and interest of those who might give. Are they comfortable explaining the proposed project briefly and answering inquiries? You have now worked through a lot of questions about the whys and wherefores of your proposed project and campaign. Give your answers to leadership in the context of the general briefing materials you will have prepared, or perhaps in a FAQ (frequently asked questions) format, or as bullet points. Share with them your work on the case. Then let's see if the questions and answers have been enough.

Give the test that appears on the next pages to yourself and your leadership.

▬ Trial Questions for Volunteers and Board Members

Part One

Please answer the following six questions in your own words. We will use your answers to find the weak spots in our rationale and to help us prepare better briefings for you.

What, exactly, does [your organization] do that is necessary, not redundant with other programs, and appealing?

What is most exciting to you about this project?

Why did you make (or will you make) your own gift at the stretch level?

What questions and concerns do you think others of your acquaintance might have for which you do not yet have a ready answer?

How comfortable are you explaining our financial statements? Are they clear and straightforward to understand?

What are the reasons for this campaign, its importance, and the urgency? What's the "elevator speech"?

Part Two

Have we done enough homework on the all the options? These are some of the most frequently asked questions about building campaigns. (Note: Please add others that fit your own situation.) Do you feel prepared to answer these questions convincingly? Yes or no.

Why build and not rent? Or why renovate a leased building instead of purchasing or building our own structure? _____

Why this location and not a different or less-expensive neighborhood? _____

Why have we chosen this [more expensive] construction solution over a [less expensive] solution? (An example: constructing on another site when adding square footage to the current site might solve the space issues.) _____

Are transportation access questions properly addressed? _____

Is this the size, structure, and use of square footage we really need? _____

If you had more than two no answers, we need a briefing and need to do more homework.

Using the Test to Prepare for Volunteer Training

The purpose of a volunteer briefing is twofold: (1) to prepare volunteers with better information and (2) to learn how development staff can better support volunteers and key staff solicitors with needed materials and information.

Ask for the test results to be returned to you in a timely way. Returns can be made anonymously. Then convene your volunteers and staff leadership to share the results. The briefing can focus on those areas in which individuals feel less secure. The session can close with a plan for providing additional information to volunteers in a manner that best suits their needs.

Thanking and Acknowledging Participants

To succeed in a capital campaign, your organization must be or become very good at thanking and acknowledging people. Volunteers and staff should do this as you go, not just later in the campaign. To succeed in a campaign, which comes on top of the usual hard work of annual survival, requires extraordinary effort. Every participant, from the line staff member who is called on for the creative new idea or extra effort to the top volunteer who is the engine of the ask, needs to be recognized.

A culture of asking will take you a long way down the road, but a culture of thanking will take you to a real celebration. Organize a thank-you ceremony at the board meeting at which study results are presented, at the leadership briefing session, at staff meetings, and at every milestone along the way.

Determine Early Funding Needs

Option One: Campaign for a Seed Fund

Option Two: Build a Campaign Chest

Option Three: Establish a Loan Fund

Option Four: Establish a Combination Leadership Fund and Loan Fund

Option Five: Use Public Bond Funds or Tax-Exempt Financing

Option Six: Use Private Bond Funds

Option Seven: Get Creative

Raising Early Funding

YOU'RE PRIMED and ready—except there's this little problem: you need more money to move ahead. Without it, you're stuck.

Determine Early Funding Needs

To help with this exercise, refer to the chart in Exhibit 3.1 in Chapter Three. First, determine your early funding needs. Put your budget on a time line, and estimate your near-term, out-of-pocket costs. Next-up purposes for which you may need funding include

- More planning work
- Case and literature development and production
- Campaign and support staffing
- Preliminary prospect research
- Campaign office software and equipment
- The capital project: architects, engineers, final drawings, permits
- Anything else you need to pay for soon

Put your cost estimates in the appropriate year column on your chart. You may want to set up your chart to show anticipated expenditures in half years or even quarters.

Next, review your options for developing funding against your initial expenses.

Option One: Campaign for a Seed Fund

In essence, this is a minicampaign conducted before the main campaign gets under way. First, set a goal equivalent to the costs you estimate you will need through the next several months to a year. Then organize a focused, quick campaign to solicit special gifts from key sources:

- Your board and selected other individuals

- Foundations that fund capital and equipment gifts (make sure you can return to them later during the main campaign)

- Foundations that "do not fund capital campaigns" but might support some of your soft costs for building the development department, developing a case statement or strategic plan, or conducting the feasibility study

Nine steps to preparing a seed fund are as follows:

1. Secure the unqualified support of the executive and board leadership for such a fund.

2. Select a very small group of solicitors. The executive director may be one. All others should be prepared to make their own seed fund gift first.

3. Prepare a fund plan, including budget, cash flow projections, and time line.

4. Set a goal.

5. Decide on a recognition program for donors. For example, add all early gifts into whatever may be given later for recognition in the campaign. But consider doing something special for these "equity" donors, whose gifts will have leveraged the entire project and campaign.

6. Develop a simple prospectus for the fund. For many organizations, a letter may be sufficient at this stage, accompanied by an executive summary of the feasibility study report and a few choice images and testimonials you have collected.

7. Select a limited number of prospects (ten to twenty) to approach. Decide on an amount to ask for: fixed or flexible?

Now let's find out who your prospects are.

Prospect List for a Seed Fund

	Name	Ask Amount	Estimated Amount
1.			
2.			
3.			
4.			
5.			
6.			
7.			
8.			
9.			
10.			
11.			
12.			
13.			
14.			
15.			
16.			
17.			
18.			
19.			
20.			

Goal = $_____   Ask Total = $_____   Est. Total = $_____

8. Seek a meeting with each prospect and ask for a gift. Remember, the purpose of the fund is to mobilize ready money.

9. Hold a small celebration and thank-you party upon meeting your goal.

Option Two: Build a Campaign Chest

Fund the costs out of a campaign chest that you have saved for over the years in the form of retained revenues or special gifts. A school in San Francisco called it the "Dare to Dream Campaign." It was the focus of early appeals for three years prior to the campaign.

Option Three: Establish a Loan Fund

The third option is for relatively few organizations. The following types are good candidates:

• *Type A:* Your organization is well ensconced in a larger one with the resources, confidence, and commitment to proceed. (Examples: an institution at a large university; a clinic within a large hospital)

• *Type B:* You have impeccable credit and secure-enough funding within view to convince a commercial lender.

• *Type C:* Your organization qualifies for a loan under the terms of a special nonprofit loan program. (Example: the New York–based Nonprofit Finance Fund, with several planning grant and loan offices located around the country)

Option Four: Establish a Combination Leadership Fund and Loan Fund

Raise some; borrow some. You may be able to supplement the money raised from a seed fund campaign with borrowed funds. Sources of loan funds could include your own organization's cash reserve or quasi-endowment (never the endowment fund), an interested institutional lender, or an individual.

Option Five: Use Public Bond Funds or Tax-Exempt Financing

This is money you don't pay back. Public bond revenues are the reward of long, advance work—often two to five years and repeated attempts. Large organizations may be able to get their own issue on a ballot; bonds benefiting a group of organizations are more common. Shifting political winds make relying on this type of financing perilous. However, the proceeds can be well worth the trouble. Many civic organizations are able to raise a significant part of their projected costs with the proceeds from a public bond issue, either local or state.

Here are two scenarios to investigate:

1. Members of your organization are well connected and can help get your organization included in a popular omnibus bond measure. You put in relatively little work campaigning for the bond measure, and the voters send you lots of money. Congratulations.

2. Members of your organization, both volunteer and staff, work hard to assess the climate for a bond measure on your behalf. You hire an advocacy firm to do the professional leg work; they give you a favorable report for an amount of money they think the voters will pass. With the help of your hired advocacy firm, you get the bond measure on the ballot and campaign hard for it. It passes. Revenues arrive when you are ready to spend them.

Option Six: Use Private Bond Funds

This is money you pay back with interest. If your organization is large enough to support a strong cash flow and has strong credit, you can investigate obligating your organization via a private bond issue. You will need to locate a financial institution that will work with you to set up a private bond issue, assuming your organization can qualify. You can expect to pay related, up-front legal and professional fees.

The size of the issue and the time table for paying it off are structured according to the expectations for the fund raising program and types of gifts solicited (unrestricted or restricted to the capital purpose).

Federal guidelines govern this process. For example, proceeds from tax-exempt bond revenues may not be used to replace funds you have already raised—whether paid in or pledged—that are earmarked to pay for a capital project. When future restricted pledges are paid in, it is possible to invest them and earn interest on them before having to make a bond payment. Your estimates are critical in setting up the schedules and commitments. Get professional advice.

Option Seven: Get Creative

Your constituents can assign assets to your organization to be managed by you for various purposes, for example, (1) to contribute some form of interest or gain on the asset or to act as collateral or (2) to help you secure loan funds.

- *Example 1: Real estate.* Your building, on which you have been paying rent, is contributed to you or you already own it. You can sell it at any point in the campaign. In the meantime, you may use the equity in the property as collateral against a loan.
- *Example 2: IRA funds.* Your constituents assign management of their retirement accounts to your organization, either for the term of the campaign or for an indefinite term. You offer a reasonable, fixed rate of return to your donor-customer, and anything the investment makes above that figure goes to the campaign.

Looking Ahead

YOU'RE ON YOUR WAY! You have done everything within reason to prepare your capital campaign, and things are looking soundly optimistic. Congratulations on all your hard work.

You are now good and ready to leave off "preparing" and move into your start-up phase. During start-up you will complete all the final steps to put the campaign formally in place and then celebrate, if you choose, with a kickoff event.

During the next phase, beyond the pages of this workbook, you will clarify roles in your campaign for the volunteer leadership, the executive director, the director of development, and the consultants.

You will also do these things:

- Confirm the goal and set a time line.

- Organize your campaign volunteer leadership structure.

- Recruit and organize campaign volunteer teams; train solicitors.

- Build the campaign plan, including a gift table and gift solicitation strategy.

- Prepare time lines and decide on milestones.

- Develop a strategy for relating your annual fund to your campaign fund activities and acknowledgments.

- Create a campaign marketing strategy, including your print and media case materials.

- Develop a campaign budget.

- Ensure that knowledgeable staff is in place to lead and support the campaign.

- Organize and staff the campaign office and establish procedures.

- Conduct preliminary prospect research; research the donor base to identify suitable prospects; use volunteer committees to help identify prospects and their particular interests.

- Develop a plan to continue to find new prospects.

- Complete the rationale and case for the campaign. Develop the case statement, written materials, solicitation materials, and the overall approach to "positioning" the campaign with your various constituencies (anyone with a reason to care about you and what the campaign may mean).

- Create a recognition program: naming opportunities, giving levels, and other ways to recognize and acknowledge donors and volunteers.

- Refine your plan for communicating with campaign committees and constituents throughout the course of the campaign.

- Obtain commitments for lead gifts.

- Plan a calendar of special events and public relations activities.

- Conduct early solicitations for leadership gifts.

- Prepare your campaign kickoff celebration.

Have a great time with your campaign. May it bring you all the satisfaction of knowing that your team has helped to make the world a better place. *Good luck!*

Resources

Top Ten Reasons Campaigns Fail

Many factors can slow or stop the flow of funds. Here are some of the biggest invitations to trouble.

1. Lack of an effective volunteer campaign chair or chairs (leadership is weak, aggressive, uncommunicative, or controlling)

2. Lack of sufficient numbers of qualified prospects

3. No institutional plan for the future

4. Lack of demonstrated need

5. Lack of staff leadership

6. Lack of experienced fund raising staff

7. Setting an aggressive goal without reference to solid information about prospects

8. Poor campaign plan: unrealistic focus, sequence, or time line

9. Poor communications and disparate groups who do not work as a team

10. Nasty surprises that stop momentum

Examples of reason 5: (1) No executive director is in place at key times, or there's no continuity in the executive position. (2) The executive is too encumbered by day-to-day operations or other program issues to devote sufficient time to the campaign.

Examples of reason 8: (1) The campaign begins with solicitations for small gifts, leaving the large gifts for later. (2) The focus in capital fundraising is on benefit events. (3) The campaign counts on too much too soon, discovering too late that it really does take an average of almost two years to cultivate a new major donor. (3) The campaign relies too much on government funding. Changes in the political climate can affect bond issues, discretionary government funds, federal grants, and much else.

Examples of reason 10: (1) The project is poorly managed, and project costs soar. For example, it may be discovered that the chosen construction site is contaminated. (2) Deplorable financial conditions suddenly come to light. (3) The top executive suddenly resigns.

Estimating the Costs of Fund Raising

According to national statistics compiled by the National Society of Fund Raising Executives, most campaign costs average between 5 and 15 percent of the funding goal. Costs include staffing, materials, office expenses, and cultivation expenses.

Campaign Goal	Percent	Estimated Cost Ranges
$ 1,000,000 to $ 4,000,000	12–15%	$120,000 to $600,000
$ 5,000,000 to $ 9,000,000	10–14%	$500,000 to $1,200,000
$10,000,000 to $19,000,000	8–12%	$800,000 to $2,280,000

These percentage estimates still depend on many critical factors, which can be divided into four basic categories: (1) readiness factors, (2) campaign factors, (3) campaign personnel and counsel fee, and (4) campaign items in the budget.

Readiness Factors

- Volunteer leadership, experience, dedication, and motivation
- Case for support
- Length of existence
- History of fund raising
- Volume and variety of fund raising programs offered
- Available prospects
- Existing donors
- Access to sources of wealth
- Focus on the sequential fund raising of major gifts
- Professional staff

Campaign Factors

- Operating budget choices
- Quality of materials
- Length of campaign
- Type of campaign
- Use of direct mail and advertising

Campaign Personnel and Counsel Fee

- Number of people assigned to the campaign
- Use of resident counsel
- Type of service offered by campaign counsel
- Public relations

Campaign Budget Items

- Salaries

  Campaign director

  Campaign assistant

- Consultants

  Fund raising

  Public relations

- Special campaign materials

  Case statement, inserts, response cards

  Video

  Donor recognition

  Direct mail or special appeal

  Manuals

  Displays, banners, posters

  Stationery

- Public relations or promotional materials

  Graphic design

  Production, printing

  Newsletters, bulletins, Web site

  Photography

- Special events and programs

  Cultivation receptions, dinners

  Major promotional events

  Site presentations

  Volunteer training and orientation

- General expenses

    Travel

    Mileage, parking, meals

    Supplies, postage, other

    Equipment

    Telephone

    Consultant expenses

    Contingency (approximately 4 percent)

- Other
- Interior and exterior donor recognition
- Renderings

Sample Expenses for a Three-Year $3 Million Capital Campaign

In a small campaign, expenses mount up quickly as a percentage of the overall goal. It is a challenge to meet the variety of costs needed and keep the expenses-to-revenue ratio low. Increasingly, smaller organizations are launching campaigns under $10 million. This expense list suggests how the necessary costs might fall. Larger campaigns would scale up and add many other costs associated with communications and cultivation.

	Year One	Year Two	Year Three
Salaries and Benefits			
Executive director (not counted)			
Staff campaign coordinator	$45,000	$45,000	$45,000
Support staff	35,000	35,000	35,000
Consulting fees	45,000	30,000	25,000
Design, production, other	20,000	5,000	5,000
Campaign travel	500	500	250
Equipment	500	n/a	n/a
Campaign brochure	3,500		
Campaign synopsis	750		
General campaign mailer			8,000
Pledge card	450		
Quarterly newsletters	2,000	2,000	2,500
Other printing	500	500	500
Postage	1,000	1,000	2,000
Other	1,000	1,000	1,000
Total Expenses	$155,200	$120,000	$124,250

Percentage of Goal Spent
for Campaign: 13%

Organizations

Council for the Advancement and Support of Education (CASE)
11 Dupont Circle, Suite 400
Washington, DC 20036
(202) 328-5900

CASE sponsors a national conference on fund raising for schools and universities. Publications and support specialized for education-based fund development.

The Foundation Center
79 Fifth Avenue
New York, NY 10003
http://www.fdncenter.org

National Center for Non-Profit Boards (NCNB)
2000 L Street, Suite 411
Washington, DC 20036
http://www.ncnb.org

The NCNB provides publications, programs, and services to increase the effectiveness of nonprofit organizations by strengthening their boards of directors.

The National Committee on Planned Giving
1592 Union Street, Suite 721
San Francisco, CA 94123
(415) 567-7780

The committee sponsors a national conference in October, provides a national membership roster, has a regular newsletter, and serves as a resource for its members nationwide.

National Society of Fund Raising Executives (NSFRE)
1101 King Street, Suite 700
Alexandria, VA 22314
(800) 666-3863
http://www.nsfre.org

NSFRE sponsors a national conference on fund raising in the spring and provides a journal and a newsletter. The society operates a resource library; full-time librarians will research, retrieve, and mail copies of articles and publications to members. Chapters provide a variety of programs for professional development, regional conferences, and workshops. Check your local NSFRE chapter for links to other nonprofit service organizations in your area.

Course available: "Managing the Capital Campaign"
The Fund Raising School
Indiana University Center on Philanthropy
550 West North Street, Suite 301
Indianapolis, IN 46202
(800) 962-6692
http://www.philanthropy.iupui.edu

**Course available: "Capital Campaigns, Major Gifts,
and Planned Giving"**
Institute for Non-Profit Organization Management
College of Professional Studies
University of San Francisco
2130 Fulton Street
San Francisco, CA 94117
(415) 422-6378
http://cps.usfca.edu/certificates

Nonprofit Finance Fund (NFF)
70 West 36th Street
New York, NY 10018
(212) 868-6710
http://www.nonprofitfinancefund.org

The NFF is a New York–based community development financial institution with regional offices in California, Illinois, Massachusetts, and Pennsylvania. It offers a loan program that provides financial and technical assistance to nonprofit organizations, with a focus on capital needs.

Other Useful Web Sites

INDEPENDENT SECTOR: http://www.indepsec.org

PlannedGiving.com: http://www.plannedgiving.com

Internet Nonprofit Center: http://www.nonprofit-info.org

References

Bar Association of San Francisco. *125th Anniversary Campaign.* San Francisco: Bar Association of San Francisco, 1997.

Broce, T. E. *Fund Raising: The Guide to Raising Money from Private Sources.* (2nd ed.) Norman: University of Oklahoma Press, 1986.

Bryson, J. M., and Alston, F. K. *Creating and Implementing Your Strategic Plan: A Workbook for Public and Nonprofit Organizations.* San Francisco: Jossey-Bass, 1995.

Dove, K. E. *Conducting a Successful Capital Campaign: The New, Revised, and Expanded Edition of the Leading Guide to Planning and Implementing a Capital Campaign.* (2nd ed.) San Francisco: Jossey-Bass, 2000.

Kresge Foundation. "President's Statement." *Annual Report, 1994.* [http://www.kresge.org].

Kristof, R., and Satran, A. *Interactivity by Design: Creating and Communicating with New Media.* Mountain View, Calif.: Adobe Press, 1995.

Lederer, R. *Anguished English.* New York: Dell, 1989.

Lee, M. "Using the Internet to Raise Capital Funds." Audiotape of session EC8 given at the International Conference on Fund Raising of the National Society of Fund Raising Executives, Mar. 26–29, 2000, New Orleans. [http://www.nsfre.org].

Rosso, H. A., and Associates. *Achieving Excellence in Fund Raising: A Comprehensive Guide to Principles, Strategies, and Methods.* San Francisco: Jossey-Bass, 1991.

Schaffer, R. H. *High-Impact Consulting: How Clients and Consultants Can Leverage Rapid Results into Long-Term Gains.* San Francisco: Jossey-Bass, 1997.

White, E. B. "Introduction." In W. Strunk Jr. and E. B. White, *The Elements of Style.* Old Tappan, N.J.: Macmillan, 1959.

Useful Publications

Alford, J. R. (ed.). *Building and Managing an Asset Base: Information and Advice for Nonprofit Organizations.* New Directions for Philanthropic Fundraising, no. 14. San Francisco: Jossey-Bass, 1996. A sourcebook for any nonprofit organization, from established institutions with a multimillion-dollar budget to grassroots agencies looking to grow.

Bancel, M. "Divided We Stand: How to Go After the Diverse Dollar and Still Stay in One Piece." *Advancing Philanthropy,* 1999, 7(1), 31–35. Includes guidance for developing major donor prospects from your membership base.

Barrett, R. D., and Ware, M. E., *Planned Giving Essentials: A Step-by-Step Guide to Success.* Gaithersburg, Md.: Aspen, 1997.

Brakeley, G. A., Jr. *Tested Ways to Successful Fund Raising.* New York: Amacom, 1980. An excellent overview written by one of the most successful consultants ever. Fifty years of experience, well distilled.

Broce, T. E. *Fund Raising: The Guide to Raising Money from Private Sources.* (2nd ed.) Norman: University of Oklahoma Press, 1986.

Bryson, J. M., and Alston, F. K. *Creating and Implementing Your Strategic Plan: A Workbook for Public and Nonprofit Organizations.* San Francisco: Jossey-Bass, 1995.

Burlingame, D. F., and Hulse, L. J. (eds.). *Taking Fund Raising Seriously.* San Francisco: Jossey-Bass, 1991. See especially Chapter Ten, "My Sixteen Rules for a Successful Volunteer-Based Capital Campaign," by Alex Carroll.

Burlingame, D. F., and Ilchman, W. F. (eds.). *Alternative Revenue Sources: Prospects, Requirements, and Concerns for Nonprofits.* New Directions for Philanthropic Fundraising, no. 12. San Francisco: Jossey-Bass, 1996.

Carver, J. *Boards That Make a Difference.* (2nd ed.) San Francisco: Jossey-Bass, 1997.

Connors, T. D. *The Nonprofit Management Handbook: Operating Policies and Procedures.* New York: Wiley, 1996. Examines the day-to-day operations of nonprofit organizations in the context of total quality management (TQM) techniques.

Dove, K. E. *Conducting a Successful Capital Campaign: The New, Revised, and Expanded Edition of the Leading Guide to Planning and Implementing a Capital Campaign.* (2nd ed.) San Francisco: Jossey-Bass, 2000. An authoritative, systematic guide to planning and managing a successful capital campaign in any type of nonprofit organization. Especially useful to large organizations.

Frantzreb, A. C. "The Pros and Cons of Feasibility Studies." *Advancing Philanthropy,* 1997, 5(4), 43–46.

Grace, K. S. *The Board's Role in Strategic Planning.* Washington, D.C.: National Center for Nonprofit Boards, 1996.

Howe, F. *The Board Member's Guide to Fund Raising: What Every Trustee Needs to Know About Raising Money.* San Francisco: Jossey-Bass, 1991.

Howe, F. *The Board Member's Guide to Strategic Planning.* Washington, D.C.: National Center for Nonprofit Boards, 1997.

Howe, F. *Fund-Raising and the Nonprofit Board Member.* Washington, D.C.: National Center for Nonprofit Boards, 1998.

Kihlstedt, A., and Pierpont, R. (eds.). *Capital Campaigns: Realizing Their Power and Potential.* New Directions for Philanthropic Fundraising, no. 21. San Francisco: Jossey-Bass, 1998.

Kihlstedt, A., and Schwartz, C. P. *Capital Campaigns: Strategies That Work.* Gaithersburg, Md.: Aspen, 1997. Well-organized reference for community-based organizations about every aspect of capital campaigning, written in a straightforward and engaging manner.

Kristof, R., and Satran, A. *Interactivity by Design: Creating and Communicating with New Media.* Mountain View, Calif.: Adobe Press, 1995.

Lee, M. "Using the Internet to Raise Capital Funds." Audiotape of session EC8 given at the International Conference on Fund Raising of the National Society of Fund Raising Executives, Mar. 26–29, 2000, New Orleans. [http://www.nsfre.org].

Mixer, J. R. *Principles of Professional Fundraising: Useful Foundations for Successful Practice.* San Francisco: Jossey-Bass, 1993. Provides a rare theory-into-practice understanding of the social exchange that motivates individuals and organizations to become donors and to continue giving.

Nelson, D. T., and Schneiter, P. H. *Gifts in Kind.* Rockville, Md.: Fundraising Institute, n.d.

Pappas, A. T. *Reengineering Your Nonprofit Organization: A Guide to Strategic Transformation.* New York: Wiley, 1996. Explores innovative strategies to transform your organization effectively and efficiently.

Quigg, H. G. (ed.). *The Successful Capital Campaign: From Planning to Victory Celebration.* Washington, D.C.: Council for Advancement and Support of Education, 1986. An excellent collection of articles, principally about higher education but applicable to other types.

Raybin, A. D. *How to Hire the Right Fund Raising Consultant.* Rockville, Md.: Taft Group, 1985.

Rosenberg, C., Jr. *Wealthy and Wise: How You and America Can Get the Most Out of Your Giving.* New York: Little, Brown, 1994.

Rosso, H. A., and Associates. *Achieving Excellence in Fund Raising: A Comprehensive Guide to Principles, Strategies, and Methods.* San Francisco: Jossey-Bass, 1991. The essential guide for every successful fund raiser—covering the key elements of fund raising and explaining the profession's major principles, concepts, and techniques.

Rosso, H. A. *Rosso on Fund Raising: Lessons from a Master's Lifetime Experience.* San Francisco: Jossey-Bass, 1998.

Schneiter, P. H., and Nelson, D. T. *Thirteen Most Common Fundraising Mistakes and How to Avoid Them.* Rockville, Md.: Taft Group, 1982.

Seiler, T. L., and Grace, K. S. (eds.). *Achieving Trustee Involvement in Fundraising.* New Directions for Philanthropic Fundraising, no. 4. San Francisco: Jossey-Bass, 1994.

Seymour, H. J. *Designs for Fund Raising.* (2nd ed.) Rockville, Md.: Fundraising Institute, 1988. The first and still-classic book on general fund raising principles and practices.

Shaw, S. C., and Taylor, M. A. *Reinventing Fundraising: Realizing the Potential of Women's Philanthropy.* San Francisco: Jossey-Bass, 1995. See especially Chapter Ten, "Reinventing the Capital Campaign."

Strand, D. J., and Hurt, S. (eds.). *Prospect Research: A How-To Guide.* Washington, D.C.: Council for Advancement and Support of Education, 1986.

White, D. W. *The Art of Planned Giving: Understanding Donors and the Culture of Giving.* New York: Wiley, 1994.

Wilbur, R. H., Finn, S.K.F., and Freeland, C. *The Complete Guide to Nonprofit Management.* New York: Wiley, 1994.

Printed in the United States
79956LV00001B/129